Escape from Portugal– the Church in Action:
The secret flight of 60 African students to France

By Charles R. Harper and
William J. Nottingham

LUCAS
PARK
BOOKS
ST. LOUIS, MISSOURI

Copyright ©2015 by Charles R. Harper and William J. Nottingham

All rights reserved. No part of this book may be reproduced or transmitted in any form or by any means, electronic or mechanical, including photocopying, recording, or by any information storage and retrieval system, without permission in writing from the copyright owners. For permission to reuse content, please contact the authors at harper.chuck@gmail.com or nottingham50@comcast.net.

Photographs taken during the escape operation described in this narrative are attributed to Kimball Jones.

PRINT ISBN: 9781603500609
EPUB ISBN: 9781603500579
EPDF ISBN: 9781603500586

Published by Lucas Park books
www.lucasparkbooks.com

Contents

Introduction	1
1 A call for help from Lisbon	3
2 The reconnaissance trip to Portugal	20
3 On the road with Operation Angola	31
4 The perilous crossing into Spain	38
5 The race to San Sebastian	46
6 Five close calls	59
7 The prison	68
8 Freedom at last–crossing into France	75
9 The aftermath–Press reports, new destinations, encounters	88
10 Fiftieth anniversary reunion in Cape Verde in 2011	102
Appendix 1	104
The list of the sixty students in The Escape	
Appendix 2	109
What have some of the students become since 1961?	
Appendix 3	111
The list of participants at the 50th reunion in Praia, Cape Verde	

Introduction

This is the story of the dramatic clandestine escape from Portugal, in June of 1961, of sixty Portuguese-speaking Africans, across Spain and into France, with the assistance of CIMADE, the French ecumenical service agency. These men and women, graduate students from Angola, Mozambique, Cape Verde, Guinea-Bissau, and São Tomé and Príncipe, studying in Lisbon, Coimbra and Porto, became the future leaders of their countries after wars of de-colonization and eventual independence.

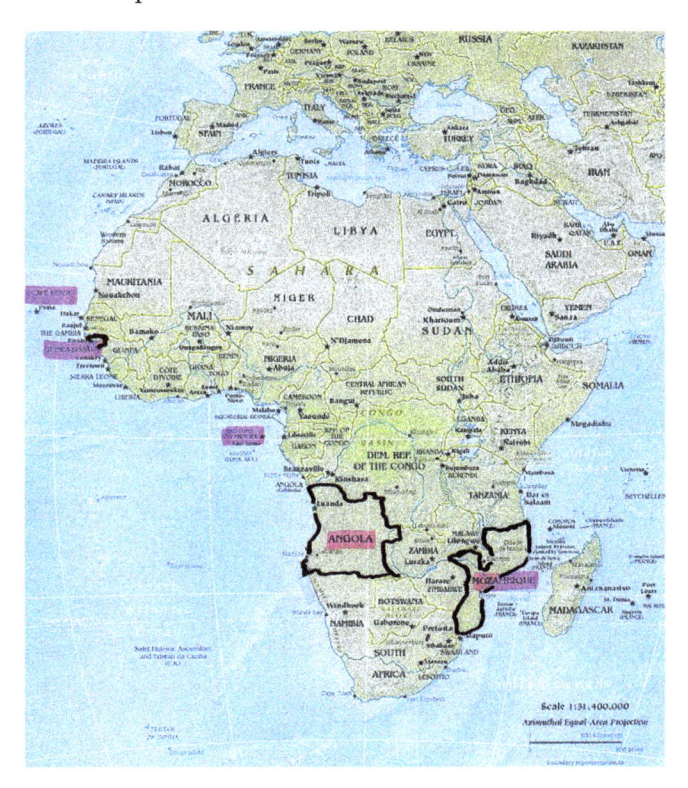

2 Escape from Portugal — the Church in Action

To tell this story, we–Bill Nottingham and Chuck Harper– have chosen to quote liberally from a series of interviews we conducted with Jacques Beaumont over the years. As the general secretary of CIMADE (1956-1968), it was he who led and energized this secret operation in mid-1961, at the request of the World Council of Churches. We were both fraternal workers assigned by our US churches to work with CIMADE at the time–Bill from the Christian Church (Disciples of Christ) and Chuck by the United Presbyterian Church USA. We were thus intimately involved with CIMADE's aims, humanitarian action and specific programs among the immigrant population in France . In developing the following narrative, we also benefitted from the detailed recollections recorded by the three American theological students who had been recruited during their summer in France to drive the automobiles with the Portuguese-speaking (lusophone) Africans across Spain and into France: Kim Jones, Dave Pomeroy and Dick Wiborg.

Jacques Beaumont, begins the narrative:

"When I met Joaquim Alberto Chissano, the president of Mozambique, at the United Nations in 1988, he said to me: *'This operation advanced the process of decolonization of the Portuguese-speaking colonies by ten years. It allowed for a whole generation to find the ways and means to prepare themselves academically and to organize themselves in the exterior, to seek financial support which is always so important to achieve decolonization, and to diversify this support'.*" "The operation," recounts Beaumont, "lasted a long time–much longer than the months we had spent together getting ready for it and carrying it out. In logical order, they comprised the preparation of the operation before it actually began. Then the operation itself was carefully divided into three stages: the Portuguese, the Spanish and the French. Afterwards, however, its sequels lasted for many years."

When he first approved of plans for CIMADE to attempt the "Angolan Operation," Willem A. Visser 't Hooft, General Secretary of the World Council of Churches, said "This is the Church in action!"

1

A call for help from Lisbon, African students, the World Council of Churches and CIMADE

By May of 1961, the growing number of graduate students from the "provinces," as the Portuguese government called its colonies, was thoroughly galvanized by the Portuguese vengeful repression of armed rebellion occurring in Angola since January. Their meeting places, in such social centres like the *Clube dos Marítimos* or the *Casa dos Estudantes do Império* ("House of the Students of the Empire") in Lisbon, came into sharp surveillance by the Portuguese political police. They were also increasingly apprehensive over harassment by the police to which they were subjected. Many had their passports revoked. Secretly, decisions were taken by the most politicized to leave the country–illegally if necessary–and to head for France and elsewhere. The incipient independence movements had neither sufficient financial means nor an organizational infrastructure in Europe to enable these students to escape Portugal.

Thus, one of the organizers of the group, Pedro Antonio Filipe, made an urgent appeal to the World Council of Churches, based in Geneva. Pedro was related to the World Student Christian Federation–the WSCF–and was part of the 15% of the students who had received primary and secondary education in Angola at schools run by Baptist,

Methodist, and Congregational missionaries from the U.K., Canada and the USA.

A mission executive for Africa of the Methodist Church in the USA, the Rev. Melvin Blake, stopping in Lisbon to visit some of these Methodist students in early May, 1961, was entrusted with the Angolans' urgent request, made on behalf of students from all five of the Portuguese colonies. The students said, "If you don't get us out of Portugal, you're not Christian!" Some other students–Silvio de Almeida, a medical student among them–who had left Portugal a year earlier to continue their studies in the rest of Europe, confirmed the request to the General Secretary of the WCC, the Dutch theologian Willem Visser 't Hooft, informing him of the daily pressures being brought by the Portuguese authorities on the students and asking for the solidarity of the churches to help them to get out rapidly.

The World Council of Churches in Geneva

The WCC, founded in 1948 at a General Assembly in Amsterdam, had been an ecumenical movement prior to and during WW II. Its pioneer founders were facing and resisting the fascist ideology of Hitler's Germany. The active engagement of Christian men and women across Europe, including ecumenical leaders in Geneva, were tireless in protecting citizens and refugees and in acting to defeat the Third Reich. Cooperative Germans were mainly participants of the so- called Confessing Church, after the Barmen Synod of 1934. This commitment prepared ecumenical leaders– such as Willem Visser 't Hooft, the Dutch first General Secretary of the WCC, to be particularly sensitive, years later, to the request of the Portuguese-speaking students in Portugal to help them escape to freedom. For example, his moral authority and leadership, exercised along with that of Madeleine Barot and other French lay and pastors, all influenced by Swiss theologian Karl Barth, produced the publication, in 1944, of the powerful *Thèses de Pomeyrol*. The *Thèses* amply reflect the ecumenical clarity at that time concerning the responsibility of Christians to protect the most vulnerable under the German occupation in several European countries and to resist the policies of the Nazis.

Responding to the students' appeal, the WCC turned to Paris-based CIMADE, an ecumenical service agency of the French Protestant Federation, asking that it take on the responsibility of organizing an escape by these men and women from Portugal to France. At the time, Madeleine Barot, one of the founders of CIMADE and still a member of its *Équipe de Direction*, held a high office in the WCC, in charge of the Desk on Cooperation between Men and Women in Church, Family, and Society. Alongside Visser 't Hooft, the two ecumenical leaders were particularly sensitive to the urgency expressed by the students in Portugal. They had to act quickly because the passports of several among them were being confiscated by the Portuguese authorities and others undergoing frequent interrogations.

According to Jacques Beaumont, "One Saturday morning in May 1961, the *Équipe de Direction* (Executive Committee) of CIMADE–Madeleine Barot, Paul Evdokimov, Suzanne de Diétrich, François de Seynes-Larlenque and I–met as usual for our twice-weekly meeting. It was at Suzanne's apartment at 53 Avenue du Maine, in Paris. Madeleine, who worked during the week at the headquarters of the World Council of Churches in Geneva, informed us that she had a request from the WCC. She reported that the WCC had just recently received the visit by a US Methodist Church representative, Melvin Blake, whose responsibilities included the Church's missionary work in Angola. He had just arrived from a visit to Lisbon. He told the WCC that the Portuguese government was actively keeping an eye on a maximum number of students in Lisbon from the Portuguese-speaking colonies (and especially Angolans). According to him, the Methodists maintained a student hostel in Lisbon, whose residents were under increasing pressure from the PIDE, the political police of Portugal. In addition, the government was beginning to withdraw their valid passports. The students in Lisbon were "fed up" with this treatment and wished to leave the country. Would the WCC help?

6   *Escape from Portugal—the Church in Action*

CIMADE in Paris

The decision of the WCC to turn to CIMADE was based on the vast experience which its team members (*équipières* and *équipiers*) had accumulated in clandestine action carried out during the Second World War. The remarkable history of this organization, born out of the courageous efforts of French Protestant youth movements to protect Alsatian refugees from the onslaught of invading troops of the German army in 1939, was rapidly followed by vital assistance inside forced internment camps in Southern France. In the early years of the war CIMADE applied a unique kind of *présence* in such camps, whose inmates came from groups of society considered "undesirable elements" by the French pro-German Vichy government: Spanish Republicans who had fled the Franco regime, German citizens who resisted the Third Reich, gypsies (Roma *gens de voyage*), homosexuals, the handicapped and–above all–Jews. CIMADE team members helped many to escape these camps, fabricating identity papers when needed, some with ingenious sculptured stamps carved out of potatoes with uncanny accuracy.

CIMADE originated in 1939 as a coordinating body of French Protestant youth movements–the French Federation of Student Christian Associations (FFACE), the French chapters of the YMCA and YWCA, Boy and Girl Scouts–as they acted to accompany families fleeing the German occupation of Alsace to the western French departments of Gers and Dordogne. The strong women lay leaders like Suzanne de Diétrich, Violette Mouchon, Jeanne Merle d'Aubigné and Madeleine Barot worked alongside French Reformed Pastors Marc Boegner, Charles Westphal, and George Casalis. The theological underpinning of resistance to Nazi and French Vichy ideology can be detected in its earlier roots in the historic Huguenot struggle for survival in the 17th and 18th centuries– and more recently (1934) inspired by the Barmen Confession. Actions were taken by CIMADE to protect French and other Jewish children and adults, thus acquiring valuable experience in accompanying Jewish children clandestinely across the border from France to Switzerland during WWII.

It was one of the first non-governmental organizations to set up a permanent presence in several camps maintained by the French Vichy government. These camps, located for the most part in Southern France, forcibly interned political opponents of the Nazi Regime, Republican refugees from Franco's Spain, French communists, Jews and other political "suspects".

After WW II, CIMADE assisted displaced persons from Eastern Europe, including Russian exiles, Hungarian "freedom fighters," Albanians, as well as Vietnamese refugees and Algerian political leaders. In the early 1960s, CIMADE was heavily involved in assisting the Algerian population to endure the ravages of the 1954-62 war of independence from France, as well as living amongst Algerian immigrant families in *la France metropolitaine*.

Part of the Equipe de Direction in Paris: Left to right: Jacques Beaumont, Véronique Laufer, Madeleine Barot, Suzanne de Diétrich and André Rouverand

Madeleine Barot, former General Secretary of CIMADE, was subsequently recognized by *Yad Vashem*, the Holocaust Martyrs' and Heroes' Remembrance Authority in Jerusalem, as being among the "Just"–those non-Jewish individuals and organizations which performed unusual and heroic acts of courage to protect members of the Jewish community during WWII. After WWII, displaced persons and refugees were the responsibility of CIMADE in cooperation with the WCC. Many of these young men and women in CIMADE emerged as part of a new generation: ecumenically-minded, honed by an acute spirit of solidarity and justice. This generation listened carefully to the urgent voices coming out of European colonies–and not only those under French control like Algeria or in central Africa.

True to form, in later years and to the present, CIMADE spoke out in defense and took strong action in favor of sub-Saharan Sahel populations, of Chilean and Brazilian victims of military repression, of Haitians, and of Palestinians under Israeli occupation.

The CIMADE leadership in Paris was thus open, experienced, and ready to take on the job. By 1961, political and social tensions arising from the upheavals caused by this civil war (1954-1962) in Algeria were almost at their bitter peak in France. Only the policy and prestige of a Charles de Gaulle, then president of France, would lead to the recognition of the legitimacy of an independent Algeria. It was for this reason that a so-called "Angolan operation" was conceived in strict secrecy. It was an attempt, in June of 1961, to smuggle as many African students as possible out of Portugal, then ruled by the dictator Antonio Salazar, and transporting them across Franco's Spain, a dangerous haven for right-wing opponents to Algerian independence, and into France.

The first preparations

By May of 1961 the General Secretary of CIMADE, Jacques Beaumont, on behalf of the WCC, flew to Lisbon to discretely meet the leaders of the students. One hundred students wished–and needed–to leave immediately as they were sympathetic or already committed to the embryonic liberation movements taking shape in their African countries.

These 100 were highly motivated and, in a real sense, constituted an intellectual elite. Among them at least three men were carrying out their military service as officers in the Portuguese army based in the *"Metropolis"*–and feared that they might be shipped overseas to fight against their own people. The Portuguese PIDE (*Polícia Internacional e de Defesa do Estado)*, the notorious political police, kept a close eye on the students themselves, deeming them a threat to Portuguese unity and suspecting them to be complicit with the rebels in the colonies. Of the total group who finally made the trip from Portugal to France, 95% were Angolans.

Total silence covered the operation. The French Foreign Minister, Maurice Couve de Murville, himself a trusted member of the *Eglise Réformée de France*, was alerted to the upcoming operation through Pastor Marc Boegner, president of CIMADE and of the Protestant Federation of France. He was also a member of the prestigious *Académie Française*. President Charles de Gaulle, informed of the upcoming operation, tacitly approved of it –but it was a delicate situation: As a member of NATO, France could hardly grant official refugee status to citizens of an ally, Portugal! Thus, safe passage of the students for an undetermined amount of time through France was authorized.

At the same time CIMADE was heavily committed in Algeria with teams in the Eastern and Central urban centers of the country, carrying out social and humanitarian assistance among the local populations in the midst of the war for independence. This highly sensitive and controversial role meant that CIMADE-Paris had to maintain discretion with regard to its operation in Portugal. No-one in CIMADE's teams involved with the Algerian events or population was informed of the upcoming *fuga* (flight) until it was all over.

Phase One: the CIMADE team gets to work

On Jacques' return from Lisbon to Paris in mid-May the plan was drawn up: One team of four persons would be on call and work out of CIMADE's offices in Paris. After recruiting some drivers for the Spanish part of the escape, the team would obtain new but blank passports to hand to the potential escapees as they crossed from Portugal to Spain. This Parisian-based team would remain on alert (*en permanence*) in the CIMADE offices on a 24-hour round the clock basis to monitor and ensure communications with the two other teams in Portugal and in Spain. Véronique Laufer, André Rouverand, Yvonne Trocmé and Marie Meylan were so designated. Tania Metzel, the head Protestant chaplain of the National Prison System was primed to be ready to meet the students at the French/Spanish border in Hendaye.

The second team of two persons worked out of Lisbon and Porto: the French citizen Jacques Beaumont and Charles Harper, a Brazilian-born American who was a CIMADE *équipier* in Marseille at the time and who had been appointed for a three-year term as a fraternal worker of the Presbyterian Church USA. These two coordinated the escape plans with the student organizers in Lisbon, renting and driving high-powered automobiles and setting up contact points for the stealthy night-time dash through back roads to the northern towns of Coimbra and Porto–and then to the river border with Spain.

A key back-up person in Lisbon was Lewin Vidal. He was a former classmate of Jacques in the French Student Christian Federation–*La Fédé*. Enjoying power of attorney status in the Portuguese-French Bank, Vidal, in effect, played the role of a Dr. Jekyll and Mr. Hyde: above reproach as a leading banker during the day but sneaking out at night to guide certain actions, keep a sharp eye out for the police, and provide valuable advice on local conditions. (Two years later Vidal would be arrested and imprisoned in Lisbon for his participation in the operation.).

The third CIMADE team was assigned to Spain. Bill Nottingham, also an American fraternal worker sent by the Disciples of Christ Church to work with CIMADE as one of its Associates to the General Secretary, headed this team. Earlier, in Paris Bill had recruited Kim Jones, Dave Pomeroy and Dick Wiborg, three American students who were in Paris at the time, as his *chauffeur* teammates. This team would work out of Pontevedra, in Galicia just north of the border between the Portugal and Spain. After hiring large automobiles in France–near the Spanish border there, they were to drive across Spain to meet at a secret location along the border with Portugal where each small group of students, having crossed the *Minho River* border into Spain, would be hiding. Their job was to drive the escapees over the 800 miles of tough roads back across northern Spain to San Sebastian–and from there across the border with their charges into France.

Three American drivers

Bill Nottingham was in his office at CIMADE in Paris on Friday, June 9, 1961, when two students from Union Theological Seminary came in and introduced themselves. Dick Wiborg and Dave Pomeroy were in Europe for an ecumenical work camp of the World Council of Churches and had been told in New York that CIMADE could help them if they needed anything. They had a couple of weeks before the work camps started and had the idea of touring France on motor bikes, if we could help them rent some. They talked about Union and about CIMADE and France.

Jacques Beaumont called Bill into his office to say that he had something to ask to which he could say "no" if he wanted or needed to, and then went on to say that CIMADE was being asked by the World Council of Churches–at the urging of the American Methodist Church–to spirit some Angolan students out of Portugal. It would be a clandestine operation and perhaps dangerous, which is why he could decline to take part. Bill pointed out that he and his wife Pat had been sent to work as *équipiers* of CIMADE by their church the Disciples of Christ and there were no conditions on that. Since 1958 they had already taken plenty of risks, including the work camp in Algeria for Bill. Pat was fully supportive. He did not know it, but as noted above, Jacques had already flown to Lisbon two weeks earlier to meet the leaders of the African Portuguese-speaking students.

Nottingham went back to his office and found Dick and Dave waiting for news about their motorbikes. He said, "Do you guys have drivers' licenses?" This surprised them, but they replied, "Oh, yeah!" They got out a map of Africa and Bill let them in on the proposition. Dave later wrote that he wanted to say, "We'll think about it", but Dick said, "We'll do it." Bill said, "Come back Tuesday, and we'll see if this thing is going to go." As the adventure grew and the theological discussions multiplied in the weeks ahead, it was to take on a meaning that would last a lifetime.

Jacques went on to say that Pastor Marc Boegner, president of CIMADE, and of its Executive Committee, had received a message from Willem Visser 't Hooft and Madeleine Barot in Geneva. Melvin Blake, the Africa secretary for the Methodists in the U.S., had been to see them after stopping in Portugal during the month of May 1961 to visit students on Methodist scholarships, there from the Portuguese colonies. They met at the Protestant seminary located in Carcavelos, near Lisbon. (Years later, in the US, Bill met Kenneth Goodpastor who was a Presbyterian fraternal worker in Carcavelos at the time of the *Fuga* Operation and told Bill that he had found one morning that everyone had disappeared! He told Bill about the arrest of the Scottish executive C.W. Scott of the Evangelical Missionary League, a former Baptist missionary in Angola, who had been erroneously evicted from Portugal after the *Fuga* was over, because of our actions. He had known nothing about it. Bill was relieved to hear that other church leaders in Portugal were glad to see him go!). Jacques explained that the students were agitated over events taking place in Angola. The war of independence had started that spring and drawn the attention of Adlai Stevenson, U.S. Ambassador at the U.N. for the Kennedy administration. As noted above, the students were being harassed by the Portuguese police and the secret police (*PIDE*), refused travel visas, kept under surveillance, etc. One of them had wanted to go to a church camp in England and was told Africans didn't need to do that. Others felt that as the struggle increased in the colonies, they would be easy targets not only for the dictator Salazar but also an infuriated public.

Visser 't Hooft had told Blake that the World Council of Churches could not do things like that itself but that

CIMADE had the skill and the experience to carry it out, dating from the Second World War, when they smuggled Jews and others out of France. So word had come to Jacques through the Executive Committee of CIMADE to study the situation, and he was letting Bill in on it. It would require a fleet of cars to move an unknown number from the Portuguese border about a thousand kilometers (800 miles) to the French crossing near Biarritz. Bill was to start putting together a team of drivers. Jacques was going to recruit Chuck Harper from the CIMADE team in Marseille to go with him to Lisbon, because Chuck had been reared in Brazil and spoke Portuguese as well as French and had lived with Angolan students in Lisbon for a year 1956-57. It was exam time in France, so Bill knew it would not be easy to find young drivers. Furthermore, in 1961 there were still relatively few experienced drivers among French students. It was expensive to own a car, and lessons from a driving school were required by law. For example, Jacques had just learned to drive when the Nottinghams got to France in 1958 and drove very much like a beginner. Bill needed people he could count on to drive day and night on all kinds of roads and in any weather, able to deal with the unexpected.

A secret meeting in Leysin

That Monday, June 12, Jacques and Bill flew to Geneva, rented a car, met Chuck Harper at the airport, where he had flown in from his shortened vacation in the USA, and went to a meeting coincidentally being held by the World Council of Churches (WCC) in the Grand Hotel of Leysin near Montreux to secure final agreement. Their arrival was all hush-hush, but Charles Arbuthnot, representative in Europe of the Presbyterian Church USA, had to be consulted and informed concerning the involvement of Charles Harper, the fraternal worker of the Presbyterian Church USA and to coordinate communication with Michael Testa, then on home leave in the US from his responsibilities as dean of the seminary where Angolan students lived in Carcavelos. The meeting in Leysin, which was organized on the theme of migration, was chaired by Leslie Cooke, director of WCC's Division (later named the Commission) on Interchurch Aid, Refugee and World Service. He took up the challenge immediately.

Jacques' narrative continued: "I laid out the situation in Portugal for them, underlining that, in the first place, the African students were being increasingly persecuted. Secondly, that this particular intellectual generation possessed a keen sense of mission and responsibility, and, in the third place, all of the students–and not only the Methodists– should be given a chance to flee from Portugal. (I did not hide that several were members of Communist–including Maoist–persuasion among them). Visser 't Hooft backed me up here, by saying that ' this is the Church in action'! At that point Leslie Cooke then raised three questions: a) how are you going to carry it out? b) how many students are involved? And c) how much will it cost? To which I answered: 'I don't know, but what I do want is a guarantee that we can count on you.' "

Also present were Eugene Smith, head of the Division of World Mission of the Methodist Church in the US. Then and there, Smith said: "We'll pay"–and in fact the American Methodists did pay–almost the entire operation. By coincidence, Mr. Smith's daughter, Lu Ann, had participated in a summer work camp run by CIMADE on the outskirts of Marseille from January to March 1961. Her positive experience there, working among the children of immigrant families alongside the CIMADE resident team, meant that Eugene Smith was already well acquainted with CIMADE and its open, ecumenical style of operation

Scholarships for anybody we might succeed in bringing out were promised by the WCC scholarship office, and the office for refugees would help. Not only would a legal status of temporary *séjour* in France be needed (Pastor Boegner would use his influence with Charles de Gaulle's Minister of the Interior) but also support had to be arranged and paid for at CIMADE's student hostel at Sèvres, outside Paris, for an unknown number of students to be lodged for an indefinite time and for opportunities for university studies. Walter Sikes of Bill's church, professor of social ethics at Christian Theological Seminary in Indianapolis, happened to be at that

Leysin meeting and showed his approval.

Jacques: "I thus returned from Leysin to Paris with a blank check. At the time, CIMADE enjoyed a healthy cash flow situation, due to our work in Algeria. We were therefore able to advance considerable sums of money for the Portugal operation, as needed, and were later reimbursed by the Board of Missions of the Methodist Church based in New York City. They were *"impeccables"* (true blue, "cool") when we sent them the final bill! Two years later at a meeting in Washington which was held under the auspices of President Jack Kennedy, I was witness to the representative of the Methodist church 'admitting' to having contributed heavily to cover the costs of the project."

Theological and solidarity motivations

According to Jacques Beaumont, the word "de-colonization" was never uttered by the American church leader in Leysin. "I felt that the motivation for the Methodist involvement in the clandestine operation was based purely on *diaconia*, with no political context in mind. However, I admit that American Methodists "quickly understood the problem, wanted to act but did not immediately know what to do." As we will see below, however, those Methodist and United Church of Christ missionaries working on the scene in Angola did see and fully understood the peoples' overall struggle for independence as being a legitimate aspiration, as did a substantial number of British Baptists. Many missionaries publicly criticized the repressive actions (including the use of torture) perpetrated by the colonial powers against the Angolan population. For that the Portuguese government severely criticized the missionaries for having trained many of the intellectual leadership of the Angolans' movements and for having been sympathetic to their cause.

Beaumont's own personal position was one which "saw this operation as a step towards the independence of African colonies–Algeria, Senegal, the Camerouns,–and now of the Portuguese colonies". He felt that it was therefore imperative that he convince some of the other members of

CIMADE's Executive Committee (*Equipe de Diréction*), of the importance of responding to the request from the WCC that CIMADE carry out the operation on its behalf. For Suzanne de Diétrich, "resolutely anti-colonialist", the option was clear. As for Paul Evidokimov–the White Russian–he had to "reflect upon it," but when he later started receiving the first group of nineteen exiles at the CIMADE Student Foyer at Sèvres his firm actions on their behalf belied all hesitation. François de Seynes-Larlenque came firmly on board.

Jacques : « Everyone behind the operation was very much afraid that the whole thing might end up very badly. I suspected that some of the people I had met in Leysin felt that they had a "hot potato" on their hands and they wanted to get rid of it as soon as possible! In retrospect, I think that they had never really thought through the whole issue of colonization. They had not been confronted up front with the relationship between these factors: 'Christian mission', 'civilization' and 'colonization' and in my view they had never had to come to grips with the situation created in the Portuguese colonies–which was, after all, very different from that affecting Algeria and the rest of Africa. After the 400 years of colonization by Portugal, many missionaries took it for granted that these colonies were after all part of Portugal–a bit different perhaps, but Portugal nonetheless!" Thus, after a full briefing on the critical situation facing the Portuguese-speaking African students in Portugal and an approved review of the plans for the operation which had been entrusted to CIMADE, it was decided that the open-ended operation would begin on June 15th. "There was not much time. We returned to Paris the next day."

From then on, by early June 1961, the senior staff of CIMADE began preparing urgently for the overland flight of an as-yet undetermined number of Portuguese-speaking Africans. Jacques, Bill and Chuck rushed back to Paris on Tuesday, and the next day Bill drove Jacques and Chuck to Orly airport to fly to Portugal for the operation to begin. Bill writes: "When I got back to my little Renault 4-CV, my pants ripped right up the back. I went home to Fontenay-aux-Roses and stood in our apartment in my shorts while Patti sewed up my pants. We had a good laugh at the ridiculous image of the international spy!"

Phase two : the "Angolan Operation" is launched on June 15, 1961

Dick and Dave showed up on Tuesday morning. They remembered later that Tania Metzel gave the meditation in chapel that day in front of the cross from Gurs concentration camp–Luke 10:17-20. (Nottingham preached on this text also in Montpellier in 1989 for the 50th anniversary of CIMADE, the emphasis being God's grace towards us and the world.) He still had to find another driver! There was a young American teaching English in a *lycée* near Paris. He had shown up at CIMADE somehow, but Bill only had his street– no address and no phone. He started down the street late Tuesday night studying the apartment buildings and asked a *concierge* if she knew of a young American living around there. She pointed to a doorway where she thought he might find one. Bill entered and started up the stairs, looking for names and listening. Suddenly he heard voices in English, knocked and found Kim Jones and his girlfriend Margaretha painting his room. (They married in 1962.) Sitting together in his little 4 CV Renault, Bill explained what he wanted and the need for absolute secrecy. Kim agreed without hesitation. He simply dropped any further connection with the school where he had been teaching. They later laughed at the thought of the director wondering what ever became of him! As a result of the trip, Kim studied for the ministry in New York when he returned to the States and went into counseling. He was a Methodist, too!

On Wednesday the operation was underway in the CIMADE office. Jacques and Chuck left for Lisbon. False papers were being produced in the Congo-Brazzaville embassy (by someone who was fired for this, for which we received reproach from André Rouverand, but who returned to Paris as the ambassador after a coup changed his government!) Pictures were taken of African students picked at random at the *Cité Universitaire*. Arrangements were made for housing, money, tickets, etc. Legitimate letters of guarantee on CIMADE letter-head were also drafted, to have correct names and IDs after Jacques would phone a list from Portugal, to be brought to us in Spain by a CIMADE courier. (In fact, they were carried to Geneva by Robert Tobias and forwarded to Paris from there.) Other papers were later provided by the Senegalese embassy.

On Wednesday night, Bill was to hear from Chuck and Jacques. If they said, "Uncle Nicholas is dead," the trip was off. If they said he was doing fine, they were to leave for the border. When Chuck's voice announced that Uncle Nicholas was recuperating, Bill almost passed out! That night, Dick, Dave, Kim (at a harrowing last minute, as they recalled) and Bill boarded the 2nd class sleeper for Bayonne. On Thursday, June 15, they rented four cars and crossed into Spain on their way to Pontevedra and the unknown, to meet with young people who, it proved later, would play a major role in the decolonization of their countries. A simple but effective code was set up among the teams to communicate by telephone to and from Paris and between the two teams *sur place*. Familiar American baseball terminology came in handy among the Americans. Other words were more convenient for the French.

Ensuring security

In order to test the needs and viability of the operation, Jacques had left for Lisbon in mid-May without informing the President of CIMADE, Pastor Marc Boegner, of his trip. His other colleagues (André, Véronique, Bill) covered for him during Jacques' absence, in any case. At that time Philippe Jordan and Mireille Desrez were both in Algeria in charge of CIMADE's teams, and were not informed of the Portugal operation until after it was over. It was a tense time, in the midst of a sensitive political climate.

At the latter stages of the Algerian war of independence–peaking in 1961 and just before the cease fire of 19 March 1962–the right-wing OAS ("Secret Army Organization") a violent armed insurrection led by officers of the French Army, in tandem with die-hard colonialist settlers in Algiers, attempted to overthrow the government of Charles de Gaulle.

In fact, they made an unsuccessful attempt on the general's life. Among its acts were planting bombs in urban areas in Marseille and Paris, damaging buildings and affecting many civilians. CIMADE, the Protestant agency, was considered by the OAS and its allies among the French Police and Army as traitors to the French cause in Algeria. The organization's humanitarian activities were being closely monitored by the French Army and police throughout the Algerian Muslim population. Thus, any "extra-curricular" activity of CIMADE perceived by a vigilant French police as being carried out within the geographic or political domain of its ideological ally, Portugal's president Antônio de Oliveira Salazar, would thus trigger strong reactions and would certainly affect negatively CIMADE's work in Algeria.

When Jacques returned from Lisbon he went to see Pastor Boegner about the operation. Boegner had been in Leysin and had already given his agreement that CIMADE take on this operation. " Pastor Marc Boegner imposed two conditions to my involvement: One, I was never to be alone–so as to insure my protection, and secondly, that CIMADE would not be compromised in any way by 'Operation Angola' and so that the on-going work being carried out in France and in Algeria could continue." Jacques: "Given that this operation contained serious political ramifications, we also had to know who these African students were in Portugal. We already had good contacts with a parallel network of 'anti-colonialist' friends–which included a Portuguese lawyer, (we will call him Cardoso) who later became a member of the cabinet of President Mario Soares, president of Portugal in the post-Salazar period. Also we knew a Spanish jurist (we will call him Blasques), who later became the vice-minister of justice in one of the post-Franco Socialist governments." Jacques had maintained contact with them earlier and was able to count on their advice as he made his first trip to Lisbon in May. It also helped motivate his decision, in early June, to insist on "recruiting" Chuck Harper for the operation within Portugal itself, given his Brazilian background and his earlier experiences living with Angolans in Lisbon before working with CIMADE in Marseille.

2

The reconnaissance trip to Portugal, a first meeting with the colonial African students organizing committee and "Edward G. Robinson"

Jacques arrived in Lisbon on May 15. He right away headed for the student Methodist hostel–but it was also under surveillance by agents of the *PIDE* (Portugal's political police). It took two first reconnaissance attempts before he finally entered the hostel late at night (no agents being in sight). "I was led by a student to meet Pedro Filipe (a Congregationalist) who was the leader of the small group of students living there and who had contacted the WCC through Melvin Blake. Filipe told me about how they had left Angola, about the pressures they were undergoing, about the manner by which the Portuguese authorities had withdrawn their Portuguese passports and how they had requested help but that it had not come." Jacques told the students then that indeed help had arrived from the WCC, but it came indirectly. "We continued talking late into the night and then met twice again, at night. We never informed the resident Methodist missionary at the hostel. In fact, I never even saw him! At one of the meetings the group was larger, including some who did not want to leave–they were frightened–and which included some who had passports and who could leave."

Under a tree with the Africans

Pedro Filipe then arranged for two secret meetings with the coordinating body of all the students of Portuguese colonial Africa–a group strictly political in character. They met under a huge tree in a park in Lisbon–at night, as always–and they talked at length. Jacques: "I was always under the impression, as I talked to the Portuguese-speaking Africans, that there were a significant number of candidates for study at the University of Patrice Lumumba, in Moscow, asking pertinent questions about possible academic venues. I talked to one student (the one who many years later died in Beijing) who was a Maoist and who believed profoundly in that particular political option for the future of the Portugal colonies. He was a follower of Holden Roberto, very anti-Catholic. Was he at all influenced by the Methodists?"

"The members of the student committee wanted to know *who* I was and *what* motivated my assistance to them–because, after all, they were entrusting themselves to us! We had to establish a *"zone de confiance"*. So I talked to them of Algeria, of Senegal, and of CIMADE's actions there and of our involvement, with an ecumenical leader Aaron Tolen, in supporting the independence of the Camerouns. In other words, I 'sold' CIMADE." Simultaneously Jacques attempted to protect CIMADE–he said he was risking a lot by confiding in them all. It could have *estourado,* (blown up in our faces) if one of these persons, or an undercover agent among the students, had gone public or had been otherwise indiscreet.

"We parted with an agreement", Jacques said. "Those who wished to leave on this operation had to commit themselves 'all or nothing'. The basic criterion to join the group was the wish to leave, regardless of religious, ideological, or political affiliation." There existed, already in 1961, two distinct political movements working for independence in Angola: The Popular Movement for the Liberation of Angola (*MPLA*), under the leadership of Agostinho Neto; and the National Front for the Liberation of Angola (*FNLA*), under Holden Roberto, which earlier had been known as the Union of the Peoples of Angola" (*UPA*). It was only in 1966, several years later, when a separate group–splitting off from the *FNLA*–came into existence under the leadership of Jonas Savimbi, called the National Union for the Total Independence of Angola (*UNITA*). All were caught up in the ideological Cold War crossfire between America's capitalism and the socialism of the Soviet Union, within the well-known context of the huge oil reserves in the enclave of Angola's Cabinda. Yet throughout the entire operation it can be said that it was remarkable that each person and the group to which he or she was affiliated remained loyal to the interests and safety of the entire group.

Checking out the border options

After these agreements had been reached, Jacques and Pedro drove together to two vastly distant points of the Portuguese border to check out the options. Two places lent themselves to the operation: the southern coast of Portugal, facing Morocco, and the northern border with Spain, across the Minho River. In the meantime, Jacques was strongly advised by his Portuguese socialist lawyer friend in Lisbon, "Cardoso", that the Portuguese political police, the *PIDE*, had to be taken very seriously–and thus that we should not confide in a metropolitan Portuguese citizen under any circumstances. The students would pay a heavy price if the plans for an illegal flight were to become known to the authorities. The local Protestant minority churches would also suffer–such as the Methodists, Presbyterians, and Baptists.

Secondly, "Cardoso" told him that among the African group were a high percentage of Communists, a fact which raised the stakes for us, as far as the risk of exposure was concerned. The *PIDE*, being a bureaucracy, would be slow in catching on to what was happening once people started disappearing. Therefore we were to act swiftly until all the candidates for leaving had left, before the *PIDE* woke up. That, in fact, is what we did–we went so fast that the *PIDE* did not put pieces of the puzzle together, as we shall see, until about five or six days after the last group had successfully fled Portugal across the northern border.

"During this first trip, my Portuguese lawyer friend and I went, independently, to check out some professional smugglers in the south of Portugal, on the coast opposite Morocco. I wanted to test whether our African friends were right in being apprehensive about going that route–after all, they risked five to ten years' imprisonment if they were caught by the Portuguese coast guard. In other words, the stakes were indeed high for them. After we did the whole coast, we went to see some other Portuguese socialist friends–I had to call in some political "credit points" from them as I had earlier headed up a committee in France of solidarity with the Portuguese socialist cause. Their reaction was 'so-so', with arguments for and against the Morocco route. (Besides, Jacques' own father-in-law was the director of a company he owned in Morocco for Peugeot, which would have opened a few doors …) But they decided against it because it would have taken too much precious time to set up a longer, secure route by sea–from Portugal to Morocco and from Morocco to France. It was decided: we go overland, through Spain."

An indispensable ally: *Señor Martinez*, smuggler with a heart.

Before returning to Paris, Jacques was led to the brother-in-law of a man who was a major smuggler in dry goods, mostly but not exclusively in coffee, whose vast family straddled the Portugal/Spain border. We shall call his name *Señor Martinez*. His main residence was in a small village called Arcade, situated in Galicia on the Spanish side of the border with Portugal. As we happily discovered later in the operation, his house was large, hospitable and proved extremely useful, if not essential, for the protection of the Africans. As several of us later noticed, "Martinez" sharply resembled the American cinema actor Edward G. Robinson, so we called him that. "Edward G." had family links to both the Portuguese and Spanish customs police and thus controlled a sizeable part of the territory on both sides of the Minho River. Martinez' own daughter (let us call her

Isabella) attended university classes in Lisbon and enjoyed the confidence of one or several members of the political committee of lusophone (Portuguese-speaking) Africans with whom we were dealing. This was a key reason for choosing, with added security, the northern route out of Portugal.

Jacques: "We had earlier discussed the price to pay to *Señor Martinez*, the Godfather or head of the family, for taking these men and women across the border. But as the numbers of Africans on the way out kept increasing and the risks kept rising, so did the price per head. One night we felt pretty good because the smuggler got his numbers wrong and we paid for one less person. At another time he decided to load a bag or two of smuggled coffee into our cars going the other way into Portugal, which we duly delivered to one of his men under the perplexed eyes of the staff in front of the sumptuous hotel *Infantes de Sagres* in Porto!"

The search for true/false passports: how they were made and delivered

Jacques: "When I returned from the first preparatory trip to Lisbon we had to find 55 passports or other documents such as the *laissez-passers.* When I look back on this African lusophone operation–the passports, the false documents–it was clear that there were always two objectives in obtaining them: one, of course, to gather as many laissez-passer documents as possible, and the other being a personal, political one. These were obtained from Senegal, from Gabon (which borders on Cabinda), and Niger. Interestingly, Niger was supportive of the operation because it had greatly assisted the emerging Algerian leadership. Niger's Ambassador Segou in Paris was a personal friend of mine." He continues: "These were obtained, in Paris, from the countries named above and surreptitiously carried by each driver on the Spanish side of the border with Portugal– where each African received his or hers personally. Each false passport or identity paper, when handed to the new holder, contained a real photo of the recipient on it. In some few cases, a photo was taken of another African in Paris–someone vaguely resembling him or her. In all cases the name and personal data were false and had to be memorized immediately by the recipient of the document in question when it was handed to him in Spain".

Some photos had been collected in Lisbon earlier by Pedro Filipe, the organizer of the entire operation in Portugal. The collected photographs were then taken secretly to Paris and handed to CIMADE. Each was then processed by the embassy or consular staff of Senegal, Gabon, or Niger. Some of these photos were carried back to Geneva by a passing Disciples of Christ church official, Robert Tobias, who had stopped by Lisbon at the request of Madeleine Barot, to look up some of the Angolan Methodist students there. Some of the men had their identity photos shot at various angles–three or four of them–which made for some duplication, but at least they were authentic photographs! These passport photos served for the most part to process twenty or so Senegalese passports. Additional photographs, thirty or more, were taken in Paris itself, according to Veronique Laufer, by a CIMADE *stagière* (intern), but of willing volunteer Africans walking among students at the *Cité Universitaire*. These photos were then fixed to new papers prepared by the African embassies–and were collected by Jacques in mid-June on a lightning 24-hour trip to Paris. This urgent need for more photos arose when the success of the first crossing of nineteen Africans into France engendered more and more requests by Angolans and fellow Africans to leave in a larger group of forty-one persons! Marie Meylan also took some of the finished laissez-passer papers to Hendaye, where Bill Nottingham was waiting to drive back across Spain with them to Pontevedra and to the next group coming across the border.

The ambassador from Senegal

Jacques right away contacted the Ambassador of Senegal, whom he had known from CIMADE's work in Dakar, at the Bopp Center. "My intention was to obtain real but 'false' passports for our colonial Africans. The ambassador informed me that my visit was opportune since the *Ministre de Justice*, a man named Darcy, a Roman Catholic, was to arrive the next morning. He promptly invited me to a reception for the Minister, to be held the evening of the next day, to see what would happen." At the end of the reception his bodyguards were shooed away and Jacques and the Minister went for a walk in the Embassy gardens. Jacques told him what CIMADE was about to do and about CIMADE's President, Marc Boegner. Mr. Darcy then replied: "When President Boegner asks me for something I take it very seriously. We will see what we can do." "At 10 AM the next morning, I was in the Ambassador's office. He told me, 'I had to phone Mamadou Dia'–and said that he could not take the decision alone. 'How about the microphones?' I asked. To which he replied, 'Before the French intelligence agents learn to speak Wolof, they all are persuaded that we all speak only French'. A quarter of an hour later the embassy had received the authorization to issue the Senegalese passports for the Angolans.

Passports from Gabon

After that, Jacques turned to Gabon. "I chose this country because it is a neighboring state to Sao Tomé and Principe, as well as to Angola, with economic interests in both." At first the ambassador did not wish to receive him, but the consul did. It turned out that he helped CIMADE considerably to obtain some false passports. "After the operation was all over", Jacques told us, "the consul was fired from his job". The story ended well, however: when the then President of Gabon, Leon M'Ba was deposed in a 1964 military coup, the same consul returned to take up his post as ambassador in Paris. "It is true that this man became compromised by our requests that he commit 'illegal actions', but he had carried them out by conviction–in the same way that during WW II there were French civil servants who did the same."

...and from Niger

"The third country that helped us was Niger. Its ambassador in Paris–a man called *Segou*–possibly Ibrahim

Loutou–was a progressive thinker of the 1960s movement and a representative of the underdeveloped and non-aligned countries with considerable influence in Africa. He later became the senior figure among African ambassadors in Paris and became the Associate Director General of UNESCO in Paris."

"We thus worked with a small group of persons with whom we could do a number of things". Jacques reported. "In the same way, we could trust a small number of people who worked with us in CIMADE on the question of torture in Algeria. I came to realize, in fact, that this was a very small circle of trusted persons at the time".

Fine-tuning precautions

Jacques: "At that point our work was cut out for us. We had to get Charles Harper back from his vacation in the USA. We had to convince the president of CIMADE, Marc Boegner, of the importance of the operation and our involvement as CIMADE in it. As a matter of fact he was not kept fully informed of all of our operations in Algeria, but was sufficiently intelligent to suspect what they were. My main concern was to protect CIMADE and in particular its work among the Algerians. It was essential that the *OAS* (the French-Algerian Secret Army Organization) be given no pretext for threatening CIMADE. We alerted Gaston Defferre, the Socialist mayor of Marseille and a Protestant, so that he would contact Boegner in case of urgent need for information."

A code system–U.S. baseball

It was very clear that we had to establish communication codes not only with Paris, but also to be able to communicate with each other in Portugal and with the team run by Bill in Spain while they were in Pontevedra or on the road. For example to be able to tell one another that such and such an auto was waiting in such and such a neighborhood of Lisbon or of Porto–and at which street corner. We used baseball terms (such as making it to second, or striking out, sliding home…,). We invented medical conditions for a fictitious

"Uncle Nicholas" (he's sick, or out of hospital…) to inform each other and Paris over the phone on the status of the operation, warnings or emergencies.

Chuck: "Even though Jacques and I stayed overnight at a same hotel we did not want to be identified as being colleagues or acquaintances (again, not knowing if the *PIDE* was aware of what we were doing)!" "Each of us had his 'disguise'–as Jacques reminded us. We dressed differently, I as an American tourist and Jacques as a Frenchman with his wrinkled white shirt (*chemise blanche frossée*). We were so naïve, if we thought for a minute that we could have fooled the *PIDE* had they been on our tails!"

Notification to French authorities

Jacques: "When I returned from Lisbon in mid-May I went to see some French government contacts to let them in on the operation. In case anything happened to me (or us) I did not want the Algerian programs or contacts to suffer. Also, it was important that some trusted government officials were apprised of the operation to help the colonial Africans, principally Robert Buron, the Minister of Transport, responsible in the Charles de Gaulle government for negotiations with the FLN over Algeria. I also met Bernard Tricot , the *Secretaire d'Etat chargé des Affaires algériennes* (the specialist on Algerian affairs, under Buron.) I told Buron that I would be out of the Algerian picture *dans la nature* (out of touch) for a couple of months. If there were some catastrophe affecting us, 'could I count on you'? For example, to mobilize some progressive Roman Catholic bishops in Spain and in Portugal …to alert Cardinal Bellini (a high official in the Vatican), …or media people in Senegal. For me, Buron was a hidden protection. Each time I returned from Portugal I phoned both Buron and Tricot to keep them up to date. The Minister of Foreign Affairs, Maurice Couve de Murville, was of course aware of the operation (Pastor Boegner had seen to that). But we did not talk to him directly–one simply does not ask a Minister to 'cover' an operation which, in fact, is illegal. However, if something were to happen (and it did later with the detention of the 41 overnight in San Sebastian) the minister would have immediately intervened".

Jacques also maintained another contact, a member of the Communist Party who worked at the main Parisian police headquarters, the *Préfecture de Police,* a contact dating from when CIMADE worked actively during WW2 in *le temps de la Résistance* (the time of the Resistance). "This man always had helped us...let us simply say that he was highly placed at the Police Headquarters. Before leaving I had asked Pastor Boegner to 'be so kind as to inform' Maurice Couve de Murville, the Foreign Minister under Charles De Gaulle and a member of the French Reformed Church. They met, I believe, during a trip which Boegner made to Athens, to deliver a speech."

During that trip Couve de Murville gave Boegner his unofficial approval to allowing the lusophone Africans to enter into France during the operation, with a *"laisser passer"*– an official pass, or permit. The Minister did not agree to grant an automatic regularization of their presence once in France, but guaranteed that they would receive proper temporary documentation. This assurance freed Pastor Boegner, on his return to Paris from Athens, to sign individually prepared CIMADE documents, handed to each African as he or she crossed the border from Portugal to Spain, stating that CIMADE would assume responsibility for their presence in France.

"These were precious documents", Bill said. When the last group of forty-one Africans were leaving Spain and were arrested in San Sebastian–Bill being arrested as well–some members of the group did destroy some of their newly-issued personal documents. "But all kept their CIMADE guarantees (*"attestations"*) with them in detention, except for one woman who, fearful, chewed and swallowed hers!" Jacques remarked that he was later told that another "kept his Senegalese document hidden, shall we say ...in a lower orifice...

30   *Escape from Portugal — the Church in Action*

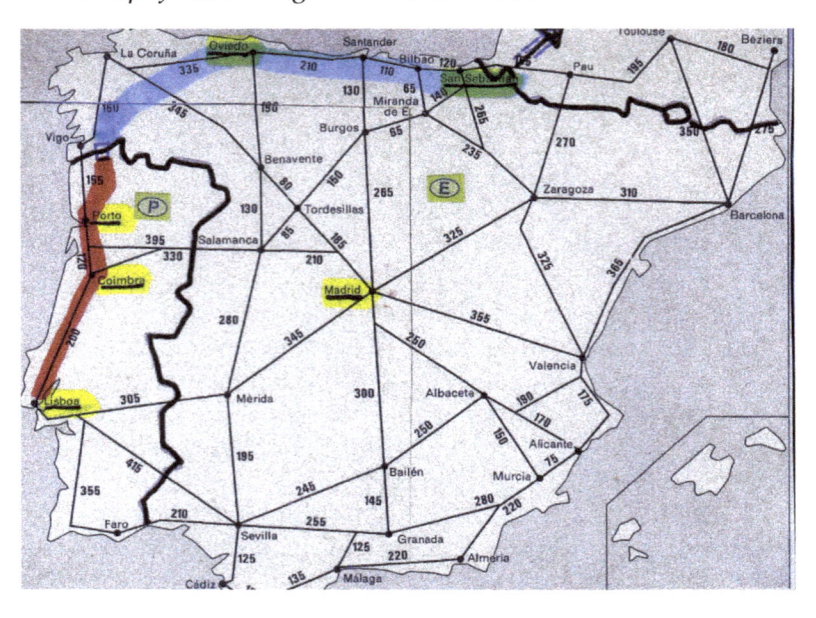

3

On the road with "Operation Angola"

A flight to Lisbon, our rendez-vous in Pontevedra, choice of the first nineteen escapees, hiding in the woods by the Minho

On Wednesday the 14th of June, Jacques and Chuck travelled to Lisbon in separate rows on an Air France flight. *"You never know!"* Jacques remarked. Around nine PM they met the leaders of the students' organizing committee at a corner in a discrete park. Last details were agreed upon: the names of those who would be driven north in the first two carloads, where in the city the pickups should be, and at what precise time. Three weeks earlier, on his first trip to Lisbon, Jacques had had long exchanges with the leaders, explaining the nature and purposes of CIMADE, its history and its motives in committing itself to the operation. In exchange, confidence had to be earned both ways: *"What guarantee is there that one of you is not an agent of PIDE?"*

Getting organized in the park

Chuck recalls that "the first thing we did on arrival was to meet that very evening–quite late when summer darkness fell–with the African leaders of the operation. They were the ones with whom Jacques had met a couple of weeks earlier. Thus we met in the appointed place in the familiar park."

"Under the park trees", Jacques added, "we found our way around in the dark with small pinpoint flashlights and protected by the guys who had been assigned to keep watch (*guetteurs*). Our Angolan delegation joked about how no passerby could possibly see them in the dark, but certainly could see us–the only two white guys in the park."

Chuck: "I was doing the interpretation, when necessary, from Portuguese to French to Portuguese. However Pedro Filipe and two or three others spoke French. After about an hour's discussion it was agreed with the group's leaders that we would test the waters by driving north with a first small group of eight persons in two rented automobiles to the northern border of Portugal with Spain. I heard one of the guys later describe the scene as 'being right out of the movies.' In fact, looking back, the whole operation was a James Bond film without revolvers (well, almost …) and without the women in furs! Jacques and I then received the list of names of who was to go with us, where, what day and at what exact time we would locate them in Lisbon, to board them in one of the two autos which Jacques and I were to rent." "In essence", Jacques concluded, "We had the cars, and they made the lists of who would go and when and what had to be done to prepare them for this perilous escape. We told them, as far as we were concerned, 'You can assign the people you want, from a starting point in Lisbon, in Coimbra or in Porto, and we will take you to the border with Spain.' "

Criteria of choice of people to make up the first group of nineteen to leave

Jacques: "Among those first 19 there were those who were less politically important but who had to leave as well. We did not go into it much since the organizers (the *Comité Directeur*) who were the liaison for this operation by Pedro Filipe, had set their criteria. We do know that there were 'heavies', the most politicized of the Angolan *MPLA* representatives, who were Catholic-origin light-colored *mestizos*, as well as Protestant blacks linked to Holden Roberto's *FNLA*, which later became *UNITA*. There were people from Guinée-Bissau and from Mozambique…. Among those first ones were some who were having difficulties with the police and had to get out urgently." Bill: "Have we ever asked if there were friends who chose to stay behind? I presume there were none who were told that they could not go, because that would have left someone discontented who might have turned them in, right?" Jacques: "There was a lot of audacity there, but a great deal of luck as well, enhanced nonetheless by good preparation and reckoning, an operation thought out to the last detail. It was very well organized, from the group's side."

The commitments made by the organizing committee and the CIMADE team had to be honored. This day, on the cusp of putting the plans into action, a water-tight agreement of trust existed between the African students. Cars had already been reserved by Chuck–two dark, heavy, ample six-cylinder sedans, a Plymouth and a Peugeot 404. He was posing as a "rich American tourist, dressed in a white linen suit. The first rendezvous was made, to meet at such and such a corner, behind such and such bar.

Driving across Spain to Pontevedra

Bill, Dick, Dave, and Kim (at a harrowing last minute), boarded the 2nd class sleeper for Bayonne. They arrived a little later than planned because of a mix-up at the ticket office, but this gave them some morning time together for conversation. The seminary students were full of questions and psychoanalysis, abstracting this involvement out of the range of CIMADE's commitment and theological understanding. They were wondering to what extent it was arbitrary and self-serving. In the days which followed, these discussions went through a dramatic change.

Arriving at Bayonne, they went by twos to the local Hertz Rental, pretending not to know each other. Bill had told them that if there was only one Citroen DS, a state of the art French car replacing the old wartime traction, he was taking it. The DS was known for its aerodynamic futuristic body design and innovative technology, including a hydropneumatic self-leveling suspension. Dave and he took off in two DSs. Dick and Kim had a big American Chevrolet and a Peugeot. At some point Nottingham procured maps of Spain, flashlights, toilet paper, and whatever they thought would come in handy. They met out of town for dinner at a Basque restaurant, flirted with the waitress, and took off separately for Pontevedra. They had arranged with a travel agent to use a *Posada* there, so they knew where they were headed. Dave and Bill stayed the night at Bilbao. On the second trip, Bill left the highway to visit the medieval pilgrimage center and 12th century cathedral of Santiago de Compostela. (He would not see it again until August, 1993, when he was interpreter for a WCC Faith and Order conference held there.)

Just before heading west, they had stopped in San Sebastian to see the Protestant minister Daniel Vidal to line up a connection for the future. Pastor Delpeche of CIMADE, who worked in France with Spanish refugees from Franco, had been in touch with him about all of this. After 800 miles of driving they arrived at the hotel, tired. They then got in touch with Chuck, in Portugal, using the baseball jargon to try to throw anybody off the track that might have become suspicious. They were keenly aware that both Spain and Portugal were fascist dictatorships and had been for decades. The next day Chuck drove legally as a tourist across the border from Portugal and joined them, with Jacques, to meet with *Señor Martinez*, the smuggler.

Chuck relates: "As we happily discovered later in the operation, his house was large, hospitable and proved extremely useful, even indispensable, for the protection of the Africans. In between transfers in Spain, before the long trip across to San Sebastian, this remarkable smuggler and his family kept the groups hidden and well fed–even putting on a dancing party to raise morale. Local girls were asked to give each of us a couple of dances to show Edward G.'s hospitality."

This was the "businessman" who was going to help us at so much per head, referring to a shipment of *los mariscos* (shellfish), recommended by his cousin across the border. Bill tells that they met the smuggler, a jovial, muscular man in an undershirt, and had dinner with him and his sons in their late teens, with his wife standing proudly alongside his chair while they ate. Bill later remarked that Edward G. paid her a compliment about how nicely she patted his cheek, to the family's amusement and her delight

Chuck returned to Lisbon and then back up to Porto to round up the future African passengers. When he called Bill after a week, he announced that they had nineteen "guests"! That was more than anyone had expected, but with four cars in Spain waiting for them, it would be no problem. On the other hand Jacques and Chuck were to have more difficulty getting them in two cars, in two trips, for the several hundred kilometer trip to the Portuguese border with Spain. There were several places en route where they could hide out so that two trips could be made. Chuck told Bill, "These guys look like the senior class at Princeton!"

The first Group of nineteen men and women

"During the next week," Chuck narrates, "in the early hours of the night, Jacques and I drove at full speed with our first charges from Lisbon, once stopping to pick up others en route at Coimbra and depositing our passengers in Porto for the next stage."

Chuck: "When we started picking up the first charges in Lisbon, there were two of our guys who waited in a bar in Lisbon. At another table two plainclothes police agents kept an eye on them. (They had been followed for several days). Having had a couple of soft drinks, our two guys headed for the toilet in the back, opened a small window and jumped out, making it around the corner in time for our auto pickup. The two agents, no doubt meditating over their *vinho verde* (new wine) might still be there waiting for our two guys to emerge from the WC. Meanwhile we sped off north to the border."

"On this first trip we were on pins and needles but remarkably calm, trying to memorize every landmark as we followed a route which was carefully highlighted on our maps (the current E01 from Lisbon to Porto, and inland on the secondary route from Porto-Braga-Monçao). We tried to go not too fast. The last thing we wanted was to be stopped by a cop for speeding. It was at night."

"During one of these trips a bad surprise caught us the night of June 23, due, no doubt, to our negligence and haste. Entering the city of Braga shortly after midnight, our cars, at a safe distance from each other, plunged into a packed *praça* (city square) full of noisy, joyous families, celebrating the annual festival of *São João*. Some delighted young men spied the African passengers in the back seat, shouting '*Pelé! Pelé!*' By the most fortunate of circumstances either the local policemen were celebrating as well or had gone home for the night. The cars gently opened a path through the crowd, as if in the proverbial Exodus' Red Sea. Out of town at last, with enormous relief, our passengers opened the side windows to the sweet fragrance of pine trees on their way north."

Meanwhile, on the Spanish side of the border, Bill and Dave were looking over the terrain from afar, waiting for instructions: when would the students come across? Dave Pomeroy recalls the moment: "I went with Bill along back roads to the farm which was owned by the cousin of one of these smugglers. It was where the Angolans were going to come from Portugal into Spain. The farm is high up overlooking a river in the valley below which is the border, with the Portuguese mountains in the background. It was just a beautiful, pastoral type of scene. Suddenly there was this almost melodramatic moment when Manuel, the owner of the farm, called out, '*Gonzalez!*' pointing down below to a small boat–a rowboat perhaps–where Gonzalez was coming across with a note telling the time they would be coming across. It said: 'The group is planning to come across tonight and will stay in a barn at the farm and you will pick them up at noon tomorrow.' So Bill and I drove back to the hotel to eat and fill in Kim and Dick, who just recently arrived." They also had stopped somewhere in a *posada* overnight along the way, because Bill had told them cost was not an issue.

Among the African students who benefitted from the "Operation Angola", a minority among them said they were practicing Roman Catholics, but a greater number (31) declared themselves to be either atheist or "Christians un-related to any church" (*chrétiens non rattachés à une*

Eglise). Nine wrote down that they were Protestants. Such, then, roughly speaking, was the "religious makeup" of a substantial part of the future political leadership in the former African Portuguese colonies !

A Basque leak–and a Basque "plan B"

Years later Jacques learned of another dimension to that need for strict secrecy, when a Protestant pastor in Pau (located in the Basque region in southwestern France) later revealed to him that on the frontier separating France from Spain–in Hendaye and San Sebastian–the true identity of the African group began to get around. At the same time a group of Basques was ready to step in and help the African students if they ran into trouble. The Basques' fierce history of independence might have constituted a key factor in the operations' success. Jacques had been in close touch in the late fifties with a clandestine *filière* (network) of Basques which had earlier taken Algerians across the border to Spain, at the request of a French *Solidarité* movement where he was active. He considered, during the operation, that this network would have been a valuable *roue de sécours* (spare tire) kept handy just in case things got hot in San Sebastian. The idea was that if things went wrong, the Basque network would take the students across the border to France.

4

The perilous crossing into Spain

The most delicate part of the operation on the Portuguese side was about to be tested: making a perilous boat ride across the rapid *Minho* River into Spanish territory. Driving from Porto, Jacques or Chuck would meet one of the smuggler's nephews at a pre-determined place on the edge of the woods along the *Rio Minho*, a bend in the road which Chuck had checked out earlier. For several nights the smuggler would guide each person down a steep path to the water's edge, then into a small rowboat. There would be a long pre-dawn wait there in a kind of flat meadow with tall bushes above the Minho River on the Portuguese side.

Chuck recalls: "Jacques or I remained with them each time until the moment they had to descend to the river. At the faint light of dawn, they started, slipping and sliding down the steep bank to the water's edge, then climbing into a small rowboat on the Portuguese side. It could take about four or five people at a time across about one hundred yards across the Minho River to the other side. Hearts pounded."

"That night", Chuck narrates, " the border guards were on double duty. About four a.m., just before dawn, the appointed smuggler on duty led everyone, single file, some of them carrying a drugged child, down to the edge of the rushing waters. The smuggler struggled to stabilize the rowboat lying deep in the water with its human 'goods'. He rowed it unerringly across the river. It landed at the 'blind' stretch of land out of sight of the alert border guards about 300 yards in each direction. These 'customers' of the smugglers, having made it across the river, had to scramble up a hill on the Spanish side without being seen by the guards on the Portuguese side across the river. A dirt path was barely visible to them. Imagine what thoughts were going through their heads! They knew us, of course, but we were no longer with them. Jacques and I were back on the other side. Here, suddenly, they were in the hands of a group of Spaniards whom they had never met before and who rushed them inside a dark barn at the top of the path–and where they had to wait for eight hours without making a sound, until *siesta* time (about 1 pm)–an interminable morning wait in the stifling, hot barn. The barn doors were shut tight. It took a ton of trust and patience–but they made it!" Jacques went down the hill to the edge of the *Minho* River once during the night, but never crossed to the other side in a boat.

There was room for only four or five people at a time. Just before dawn the boat took off at a precise point hidden in the curve of the river. The current was powerful and rapid. There was a bend in the river. If the boat had been swept further around the bend, it could well have been seen by some sharp-eyed guard in the *poste de garde* high up on a cliff. Besides, there was another guard-house up the river, also out of sight of the launching spot on the banks.

The smuggler had to simultaneously be an acrobat and a champion rower but they all made it across to the other side– even the child, Djoni, two years old, whose father, João Vieira Lopes, had drugged him to avoid being heard by the guards. Not once did the small boat get out of hand during the two weeks when the sixty Africans successfully traversed the river–thanks to the skill of our contraband "technicians" and "colleagues" in this enterprise. These masters of the Minho currents earned their living by smuggling goods–coffee for the most part–and certainly earned it those nights. Their intimate acquaintance with both banks of the *Minho* River proved to be indispensable for the success of the operation.

Chuck: "One of the things I had to do in this whole operation was to meet up with you four (Bill, Kim, Dick and Dave) in Pontevedra, crossing the legal border from Portugal as often as necessary after I had put the Africans in the hands of the smugglers the previous night. Of course I had to invent a cover story for the border police on both sides to justify my frequent crossings. (I crossed the border there and returned five times between the 17th and the 29th of June). My story was that my 'Brazilian mother', whose parents' relatives lived on both sides of the border, insisted that I pay respects and render frequent visits to them before going back to the Americas. Towards the end, I even got to share jokes with the Portuguese border police about how mothers sometimes *enchem o saco* ("annoy us with their demands"), and that I was on my way to becoming an alcoholic with which all these distant relatives had gorged me. I was always well dressed in whites, like a prosperous American tourist and behind the wheel of my magnificent 1960 black Plymouth sedan."

"The subterfuge worked, after all. It was fortunate that they neither followed me nor followed up my story, although towards the end they were getting suspicious about my frequent crossings. Each time, I either met with you or left a note for you with detailed instructions (for example about the next expected contingent and the timing to follow when you picked them up at the barn) or a message from Jacques."

They made it all within a period of two weeks–first the group of nineteen, then the remaining forty-one, across that treacherous watery border and without one single mistake! Chuck continues: "Meanwhile, after each escort to the *Minho*, Jacques and I would make our way back through the bushes to the forest road, finding our parked vehicles under the pines and would drive off to prepare for the next 'package'. Jacques would head back to Porto in his empty car. I would swing west and north to cross the official border to Pontevedra in my Plymouth, to brief Bill and his three American drivers in their hotel. I then would return to join Jacques in Porto. Bill and his seminary drivers would head for the dusty back roads of Galicia to pick up their charges at the barn above the *Rio Minho*.

During that Spanish siesta time, when ordinary Galicians, guards, dogs, every living thing and time stopped, four spacious automobiles with their American drivers came to a stop, one after another, in front of the barn door facing the dirt road.

The barn

A scramble up the other steep long bank. Now in Spain. At the top stood an isolated barn. Each of the small groups then headed up that hill in a big hurry ....and into the barn to wait for high noon. Everyone waited inside the barn–a perfect hiding place–during the long hot morning, the sun beating on the tin roof above. There were no windows and it stank with the smell of previous occupants–sheep and goats. At long last, noon came–and then one p.m.–*siesta* time for all Galicians and border guards alike.

The first group at the barn: eyes unaccustomed to the light, passports, car breakdowns

Bill Nottingham picks up the narrative: "I remember the moment when we picked up the first nineteen. I'll never forget standing in front of that wooden shed with the other drivers, throwing wide the doors and looking into the faces of 19 scared young men and women.

When the doors flew open I see the first persons emerging from the barn, packed together and with their eyes wide open not knowing what was going to happen next or what to expect. Were we the police? Or friends…? Then the stress–as they got into their assigned cars– of having to immediately memorize the detailed data of their new identities on the documents they were handed: 'Read this right away, before we pass the secondary border down the road!' Instantly, we tried to match up pictures on the false papers with people they resembled–a beard, girl with headscarf, man with glasses, etc.

Quickly we divided the students among the four cars and took off in different directions for San Sebastien. It was no coincidence that this phase of the flight took place during siesta time: in effect the border guards were asleep as the four autos rolled by. The cars were in fact separated by about fifteen minutes."

"Earlier, on our way to the barn, at the appointed hour, we took off from our hotel. I had bought a lot of oranges for the cars. I caught one of our nervous drivers carefully counting them out and yelled, ' Throw them in and let's go! ' We picked up the smuggler in my car–it was 'Edward G.'– and started down a back road following his son on a motor scooter. Dave's car had an accident on a narrow bridge, and I panicked: 'What's he going to do?' Edward G. just shrugged his shoulders and motioned to go on. Dave managed to get his damaged fender straightened out and soon joined us at the barn in the cornfields of a small farm on the river."

"As we drove up to the barn I suddenly had problems of my own. The brake pedal went right to the floor. In a moment the emergency hydraulic response took over, and I had more braking than I needed, with the car bucking like crazy before we stopped. My car bucked so badly I had to stop after a loud clatter. It was just the tire iron that had fallen out from under the hood but it scared us all further. What was happening was that the hydraulic suspension which was a famous feature of the DS, permitting it to ride high through dirt roads or a downpour and cushioning sudden stops, etc. had fed itself into the brake system when that let go.

Fortunately, my car settled down and ran beautifully about half way to San Sebastien. We were going all night, of course, and at 2:30 a.m., I believe it was, we had to stop in the middle of Oviedo because there was a funny noise every time we went over the streetcar tracks. I got out and saw that apparently all of the suspension fluid had run out and the car was riding so low the mud-guards were buckled against the pavement. Scared stiff, I looked up and found we were sitting immediately in front of the Citroen service garage which was open all night! (Not the first or the last little miracle to come our way.) We were told to drive the car in but that it couldn't be fixed until morning. We just curled up and waited."

"Taking off again, we came into a small village at the foot of the mountains where road repair closed the road one-way for an hour or two at a time. To our chagrin we pulled up to park right behind one of the other cars! I think it was Kim with the big American Chevy, who had taken a different route but had come onto the northern highway near here. So we had two French license plates, American drivers and 9 or 10 young African men in a small town where blacks were rarely seen. That was the first time I ever heard 'Pelé, Pelé, Pelé!' and had to be told who Pelé was as well as the fact that his look-alike among our students really was on a Portuguese soccer team–maybe a city team or even the national. These politically-aware students did not rate that very high, saying there were a lot more important things to do than play "football" and praised their friend for leaving with them."

"Some of the students spoke a little English but since we did not speak Portuguese, Spanish or the two or three African languages they spoke, most conversation was in French. As we had been driving, the further we got from Portugal, the more the guys relaxed until they were singing. It was very moving to hear them make up a song about being 'saved' from their oppressor."

"One of them seemed to be sick. He was holding his hand on his forehead. A student who was studying medicine explained it was an abscess common among Africans and that it could be fatal. When we stopped at the village to wait for the flow of traffic to turn our way, we were surrounded by a crowd because it was evening and there was a carnival going on nearby. One man at the back of the crowd held his little boy over his head to see *los Africanos*. We had nothing to do but wait, so I said 'Let's go find a doctor.' We walked a little ways to a house indicated to us but the doctor was not there. His wife said he was over at the carnival! We showed her this young man's head and said it was an emergency, so she sent her little boy to find his father. After a bit the doctor came and I left the two Angolans and went back to the group at the car. In half an hour or so they came back to us grinning with relief, one with a big patch on his head, the other saying what a good job the doctor had done and that he would replace the bandage as instructed, which he did from then on."

"When the time came, we drove on, letting some distance grow between us, because our third car had come up behind us before we left. For a secret undertaking, we felt pretty stupid. There was a queer sense of guilt all this time because of the deception we were pulling off with people treating us so well. Whenever a Spanish policeman signalled us directing traffic at a corner, I felt I owed him an apology."

The perilous crossing into Spain

L. to R.: Fernando Chaves; Fernando Paiva, Jr.; Maria Ilda Teles Carreira; Henrique AlbertoTeles Carreira; João Jamisse Nhambo

5

The race to San Sebastian

Kim Jones : "Bill was driving this Citroën DS with the system of hydraulic pressure fluid. When anything goes wrong with the brakes or the pressure system, it just screws up the whole works. It can really be a major repair job. He said that his brakes were so bad that every time he applied his brakes the brake fluid was squirting up on his windshield through a crack in the hood. Somehow he managed. As for me, I had five fellows in my car on that first trip. Their real names were Jorge Valentim, Silvestre Lopes, Eurico Wilson, Felipe Amado and Antonio Macedo. At first they were frightened. It was the first time that I realized that these guys had a lot at stake and that if they had to go back to Portugal, some of them were fearing for their lives, especially the ones who had deserted the army and what have you. That was the first time I felt that we were in serious business."

One of Kim's passengers on that first trip across Spain, Eurico Wilson, elaborates 50 years later: "On Sunday morning, as the car was negotiating a curve in the road, the central axis suddenly broke! We had to get the car fixed–and fast. By chance, while we walked towards the next town, two local policemen drove by and gave Felipe Amado and myself a ride. Although the townsfolk were celebrating a religious festival we finally did locate a mechanic who came back with us and took our car in tow to his garage. I still remember the livid, frightened expressions on the faces of my compatriots and of our American driver when they saw us accompanied by those policemen! It took hours to fix the car–but we took advantage of the time to get a fabulous meal at a Spanish restaurant." This was the only chance anyone on any of the trips in the four cars had a restaurant meal in Spain.

Kim said later: "Over the next two weeks, these cars– and fresh ones to replace them, like a modern version of Wells Fargo horses in western films– made the trip across the 800 miles of northern Spain on winding narrow roads along the *Costa Verde* and into Basque country. A first group of 19 students were driven all the way to Hendaye and into France. Bill had to negotiate with the Spanish border officers to let them through."

Part of the Escape fleet

June 20: Arriving at the Spanish-French border

It took 19 hours to drive with the first nineteen to the parsonage of Pastor Daniel Vidal. He advised the team to drive on to the bridge at Hendaye. Jacques and others had thought he might send us up through the mountains to smaller crossings, but he did not. The four cars arrived at the bridge. The Americans were the only ones with passports. The officer said they would have to stop at headquarters in Irun.

Bill continues the narration: "We drove back following his directions and I went into the office with all the phony papers. I forget whether the first were Senegalese or from Niger, but they were entirely official from the embassies in Paris. The gentleman who received me could not understand why there was no stamp showing entry to the country, so I had to lie that we were taking these African students on a tourist visit to Santiago de Compostela and had come by train where the customs people had failed to stamp anything. He became very nervous and went into a back room while I thumbed through my passport to see if any offenses were noted for which a passport could be denied by the U.S. State Department."

"Returning, the official motioned me to join him and I was embarrassed to go into a room that was shabby, unlike the reception area, as if I were making them expose their poverty. The man was quite agitated, repeated my story–I think there was a secretary present and an inspector of some kind–but said O.K. (all of this in French, of course) and for us to go ahead. I rejoined my group, distributed papers and passports, and we took off for the border. Without any problem we arrived at the French side of the bridge, showed the CIMADE papers claiming political asylum, and after some phone calls, were allowed to enter France. It was during these moments that I recognized the second man I had seen in the office in Irun, crossing the street on the French side behind the station. This would occur to me a week later. Marie Meylan showed up from Paris. She brought more money and maybe more true- false papers. I don't remember ever changing French francs for pesos in a bank in Spain. It was June 19, a Monday."

"We bought tickets, put the guys on the train and phoned Paris that 19 packages were being sent. This was Bayonne because we had to go back to Hertz, in any case, and turn in two of the cars which had had accidents. The owner wondered what was going on–and this was his busy season–but I had plenty of money, so we got it worked out."

"Prior to that, we had thought the whole affair was over! We went to a good restaurant, safe and relaxed in France, 'mission accomplished, thank you, Lord'–and all that, laughing and a little silly. I went to a phone and called Jacques Beaumont in Lisbon (perhaps this was during one of his quick trips to Paris, though) and he said, "Nice work. Now drive back to Pontevedra because we've got some more." I came close to pleading, saying that I couldn't turn up at the border with another bunch of Africans, but he said, *'Debrouilles-toi!'* (Work it out!). When I went back to the dining room, I'll never forget those cheerful, flushed American faces looking at me for accolades–and the shock that turned them pale when I said we would do it again! My knees were weak. No one argued, though, or said he wanted to quit."

Waiting in Lisbon for the first news of a safe arrival in Paris

Bill: "Those three or four days of waiting in Lisbon, then knowing they arrived in Paris safely, will have been a moment of intense emotion for you and the African organizers".

Jacques: "Yes, I received that first telephoned message from you to the effect that they had arrived."

Bill: "I was in Hendaye then and let you know that the *"paquet était dans le train"* (the 19 students were on the train to Paris). When you said 'Get back to Pontevedra, we're going to do it again, ' the three American drivers almost passed out!"

Jacques: "I remember very clearly when I received your phone call indicating that the nineteen had safely arrived. I was with Pedro Filipe and someone else from the *MPLA*– possibly João Vieira–and turned from the phone to say, 'They've arrived!' Immediately João said, 'Let's go with the rest of us !' "

Bill: "I'm sure that he was the father of that small child. I could never figure out where he hid the group's money, later when we were stripped and put in prison. "

Bill: "All this time the same nervous decision–making, on-the-spot communication and fast action were at a maximum level with us four drivers on the various roads between Pontevedra and San Sebastian. It started with meeting and driving the nineteen Africans to our destinations, getting them through border regulations into France and then going back to fetch forty-one new ones! Where were we to keep them between trips? That was a big problem."

June 20: Jacques and Chuck return to Lisbon to pick up the second group of Africans

Chuck: "That was a sweet taste of success when we had heard that the first group had crossed into France. The decision was made to bring more out. More meetings were held and coordination with the Africans intensified."

Jacques was upbeat: "We had successfully accompanied the first group from Portugal across the border to Spain. Chuck and I paid off the smugglers and, after returning to Lisbon, reserved large brand new automobiles, a new Plymouth and a Lincoln. It was the largest luxurious car I had ever rented! It was Lewin Vidal who advised me not to be stingy on the rentals, to give the impression that we were very rich. 'Keep your cars washed and shiny', he said.'"In the Portuguese mentality and in the minds of the police, a *Senhor* riding in an enormous automobile must necessarily be an important man, somebody powerful.' And it worked!"

Jacques flies to Paris on a quick one-day trip

Bill: "Sometime during that first period in early June you flew from Lisbon to Paris to check something with the French government."

Jacques: "Yes, I did make a quick trip. An administrative problem cropped up. I only spent three hours in Paris, at the Quai d'Orsay (the headquarters of the Ministry of Foreign Affairs, where Maurice Couve de Murville was in charge). I think it was about the status which these people were to be given as they entered France: would they be political refugees or not? All of a sudden in the midst of our preparations– which were going well–some stupid imbecile at the Quai d'Orsay had told me that the guys were not to be political refugees but rather were considered …migrants."

June 21 : An *intermezzo* in Lisbon–discrete contacts with Portuguese and US Presbyterians

Chuck: "When we were back in Lisbon waiting for the Angolans and others to organize the next group and set up the pick-up points, I decided to go see a fellow American Presbyterian fraternal worker, Ken Goodpastor, at his home in Carcavelos, the suburb of Lisbon. He was the dean of the theological seminary (of the Portuguese Presbyterian Church) in Carcavelos where I had lived for a year with Angolan students four years before. He was substituting for Michael Testa, the fraternal worker from the Presbyterian Church who was dean of the seminary but was then on home leave in the USA. Testa later told me that he was fortunate that he was not there at the time of the operation, his knowing too much about CIMADE and about me–in the event that he were arrested for being an 'associate' in carrying out the operation."

"Goodpastor was not exactly delighted to see me at the door. He was not expecting me at all. In fact, he seemed very nervous and frightened, both for him and his family as well as for the seminary when he realized what was going on–I had given him a general picture of what was up. As a result I decided to leave quickly and returned to Lisbon. Jacques and I had discussed whether I should go to see Goodpastor–e.g. I could have been followed by some PIDE agent–and agreed that it would be a useful visit in spite of the risks. In Michael Testa's absence, Goodpastor was directly responsible to Charles Arbuthnot, the United Presbyterian Church USA representative for Europe, in Geneva, so he would be an additional safety link for us and the students were anything to happen to us, needing immediate outside help. I was fortunate that no students were at his home when I knocked at the door as Goodpastor was well known in Carcavelos. Jacques felt that he must have been told by the director of the Methodist student center that a significant number of residents had suddenly disappeared earlier that month. Clearly Goodpastor knew something was up."

"Jacques had earlier met, in May, a very limited number of Portuguese contacts and put them in the know. One was a respected ecumenist and pastor, A.J. Dimas de Almeida, and a friend of Jacques', a man whom he trusted. He was a leader in the *Igreja Evangélica Presbiteriana de Portugal* (I.E.P.P.) and a professor at the Presbyterian theological seminary. He encouraged Jacques to go ahead with the operation and assured us that he would be tight-lipped. He said that under no circumstances were we to take any other member of the local Protestant community into confidence."

A background note: The Portuguese churches' milieu

Chuck: "The Portuguese Protestant churches constituted a minority church within a massive traditional Roman Catholic majority. It thus possessed a minority mentality, many members feeling loyal, with some sterling exceptions, to the State and displaying extreme hesitancy to carry out anything considered illegal, placing its fragile status in jeopardy. It was no coincidence that we chose, regarding the operation, not to bring any of the Protestant institutional churches into the picture. One example of the loyalty of at least a part of the leaderships of the local Protestant churches to the colonial policies of the Portuguese authorities, was contained in a lengthy statement issued on July 4, 1961 by the conservative *Aliança Evangélica Portuguesa* and signed by its national commissioner, the Rev. Guido Waldemar Oliveira. Published by a national newspaper, *O Seculo*, the statement takes vehement issue with international media reports accusing the armed forces in Angola of atrocities against civilians and expresses the Alliance's 'warm' support to the 'Supreme Authorities of our Dear *Patria*' in its attempts to 're-establish order in the national territory'. It must be immediately noted, however, that several younger pastors in the historic Protestant churches in Portugal, such as the *IEPP* to which Dimas de Almeida belonged, were sympathetic to the aspirations of the African students in their midst. I myself was closely acquainted with several of these leaders. However, for security reasons it was deemed wise not to bring them into the picture–as much as for their own safety as for that of the Africans' security."

"As for the non-Portuguese missionaries studying the language in Portugal before being assigned to serve in the "Provinces", none were aware of the operation, nor were their leaders brought into the picture. The British Baptist superintendent in Lisbon, responsible for the welfare of his denomination's missionaries, was carefully kept out of the picture from the beginning. His name was Cecil Scott. In July, when the operation was terminated, he was picked up by the Portuguese authorities and he just about fell through the floor. As we shall see later, he was erroneously and unjustly detained by the Portuguese authorities on the charge of having organized the escape of all sixty lusophone Africans–the *PIDE* being convinced that he was the key operative. Needless to say, he was most distressed not only because he was falsely accused but because he was known for being quite sympathetic to the policies of the Salazar government. At the time everyone wished that Scott would retire and leave Portugal! As I recall, some missionaries being trained for service in Angola then told me that his paternalistic, pro-Portuguese attitudes did not sit well with them and clashed sharply with the reports coming from Baptist missionaries in Angola "

Baptist missionaries in Angola

Chuck continues: "Scott was quite out of tune with the experience and the position taken by many of these Baptist missionaries. As the Observer (a United Church of Canada monthly magazine) pointed out in its editorial in August 1961, 'churches with missionaries in the country have made united protests through formal channels against Portuguese policies and reprisals, and appeals have been made directly to Premier Salazar. In Canada, a United and Baptist delegation protested to External Affairs Minister Green'."

Jacques intervened here: "At the end of the operation the director of the Methodist student center realized that all the Africans had left. In the first group of nineteen, there was no one, according to Jacques, from the Methodist center because had we started emptying the place then, it would have been necessary for all to leave."

Finally, there were only four non-African persons in Portugal who knew about the operation: Jacques' Portuguese lawyer friend, "Cardoso"; the French banker Lewin Vidal; the Presbyterian theologian A.J. Dimas de Almeida; and, to a smaller extent, the American fraternal worker Ken Goodpaster.

Mario Soares, the Socialist political leader of the nation after the Revolution of the Carnations in 1974, became aware of the operation only after it was over–while he was still in exile in France. He later became the Socialist Prime Minister of Portugal, appointed in 1976-1978 and again from 1983 to 1985, and was elected the first civilian President in Portugal in sixty years for a decade from 1986 to 1996. He told Jacques that this action signified a significant step forward for the entire Portuguese decolonization period, covering the years 1961 to 1986. " I have no idea whether the Angolans had had any contact with other lusophones, on the one hand, or with progressive Portuguese students–certainly some, I would think, but not many."

June 22: The return of four cars from Hendaye to Pontevedra

Bill: "So we got ready to leave again from Hendaye to Pontevedra. Dick, Kim, Dave and I rented two new automobiles from the same Hertz agency. The two Citroëns, the Peugeot and the Chevrolet which we had hired in Bayonne to fetch the first nineteen Africans, a week earlier, were in very bad shape. So we turned them in. Our procedure was the following: instead of four cars travelling together or following each other, we decided to keep clear of each other with two cars going together. We stayed overnight at Oviedo, ignoring each others' presence in the same hotel. The final destination and the point of rendezvous was to be the *Hotel Universo* in Pontevedra. The first time we stayed at a beautiful, historical *Parador Nacional*. I think we chose to stay this time at the *Hotel Universo* probably to avoid attracting attention."

Return to Pontevedra

New automobiles were rented–not without serious complaining at the Hertz agency in Bayonne over the state of those just returned. A large amount of cash solved that problem. After getting different cars for three of the drivers, they took off again, this time Kim and Bill ahead of Dick and Dave. When Jacques first met the Protestant young people who had called for help to get out of Portugal, they told him that they had other friends who wanted to leave. This included not only Catholics but people of different political leanings as well as Mozambicans, Cape Verdians and others. He told them we would take all who wanted to go on their recommendation, regardless of religion or politics. This accounted for the large number they had to deal with, now.

L.to R.: Augusto Lopes Teixeira; Dave Pomeroy; Francisco Belém Rodrigues; Carlos Osvaldo dos Santos Rubio; Mário Alberto Clington; (crouching) Pascoal Manuel Mocumbi

Joaquim Chissano's experience during that trip

Joaquim Alberto Chissano was a young student in Lisbon and was persuaded by Pedro Filipe to leave in this second group. His recent published memoir after he completed his two terms as the elected president of Mozambique, tells in detail part of his own experience as a participant in the escape.

It was a beautiful day. The sky rendered Lisbon a splendor which any nostalgia (saudade) fully merited. We necessarily carried this remembrance of Lisbon with us–including that memory of a humble existence–but had to suppress it because, at the time, it was the capital of fascism and colonialism–the bastion of oppression.

Following strict instructions, I took a streetcar to the right stop, then a taxi when no-one was looking. I told the driver to take me to a bus stop by some buildings that Pedro Filipe had described to me. He had talked in vague terms in case any one of us had been accosted by a PIDE agent. Nothing had been written down. "Go to the Avenida da República where there is another bus stop. There someone will be waiting for you. Continue by taxicab to the Caminhos-de-Ferro Norte railroad station. Get on the noon train for Porto." I wanted to know if the person I was to meet was black or white, fat or thin, tall or short, man or woman. "Not important", he said. "You'll recognize the person". "What do I say to him?" I asked. "Nothing. If you are not spoken to, don't say anything. By the time you arrive midway at the Coimbra railroad station someone will be there to show you your way–but continue on the same train to Porto".

The taxi stopped. The man I then saw seemed vaguely familiar to me–it was Henrique Santos, later known as "Onmabwa", an Angolan. We both continued in silence in another taxi to the railroad station, where he promptly dropped me.

To tell you the truth I was frightened, looking left and right. I couldn't see anyone else I knew in that huge crowd milling around. I jumped into the train–but it couldn't be a first-class car–a student could hardly pay for such luxury. Well settled in a second class coach, I finally rolled into Coimbra–but again, no one recognizable in sight up and down the platform or on the train.

Arriving at a railroad junction suddenly almost all of the passengers in my coach car got off. Severely worried, I wondered if we had arrived at Porto. It finally dawned on me that we had to change from one car to another–this one was due to go off in another direction ! So it was with relief that, after some tentative exchanges with the only other Black in the new coach destined for Porto, I discovered that he was the one I was supposed to meet. He turned out to be Pastor Zacarias Cardoso, one of the Protestant students whom I had earlier seen during a visit to the Lar, where Pedro Filipe lived.

We were in the last coach of a long train, so we descended and walked a good distance to the exit of the Porto main station. Coming towards us on the platform, a man approached us and rapidly whispered "Café da Paz, at 15h00" while passing us. Later, already in Spain, we found out his name: José Carlos Antonette, another Angolan. Near the exit we passed another preto claro (light Black), almost a mulatto, who greeted us and repeated the same whispered message. It was António Madeiros, from São Tomé e Príncipe.

Chissano then joined others in the group at Porto, where they waited to be picked up by Jacques and Chuck for the second leg towards the border with Spain, in large automobiles.

Chissano: crossing the Minho River was dramatic!

We had to be careful. Above the river, waiting, we were forbidden to cough, laugh or talk–because the border guards on both sides of us were close by. The crossing point had been well chosen but we could not be too careful. Making it across the river was decisive. We had to check that nothing on us could give away our identity : things like a document or a letter, even any item like a revealing label on a lining or collar. Those who obeyed these instructions ripped off their "Made in Portugal", Largo do Rato, or Lisboa labels. I had a green suit on, brought from Lourenço Marques. Inside its greenish pockets I had letters from Carmen, some snapshots and ID papers. All this had to be destroyed and sunk in the river while we crossed it. I opted against tearing it all up but instead carefully folded the papers inside a handkerchief, along with a fairly heavy stone. The idea was to keep it in a safe place–giving myself the impression that these items could be forever kept there on the river bed, as one does when burying a loved one.

Not all of the colleagues were that disciplined: some complained of the cold, coughed or lit cigarettes–immediately snuffed out with a sharp reprimand. Or stood up, paced back and forth, making dry leaves on the ground to crackle.

The river

It must have been when the border guards were dead asleep. The first group crossed. And then it was our turn. The rowboat was too small for the number of passengers it took. But that isn't what turned this crossing into an odyssey: all of us became alarmed at the amount of water leaking into the boat. To the extent that the bottom started to fill we had to scoop its contents into a handy can on board–but making sure that it was poured overboard without a splash. Our guide skillfully used his oars to get us to the other side of a river that wasn't that wide, but the strength of the current was such that it kept us from reaching the opposite bank for fifteen or twenty minutes.

The handkerchief, the letters, the photographs and the stone ...did end up somewhere at mid-point of our crossing. But did they reach bottom? I'm sure they did not...That current dragged, polished and wore down stones much larger than mine–turning and grinding them, finally, into sand.*

---

*Excerpts above are from Chissano, Alberto Joaquim, *Vidas, Lugares e Tempos* (Alfragide, Portugal: Texto Editores, Lda, 2010), capítulo VIII, unofficial translation.

6

Five close calls

L. to R.: Antonio dos Santos Pinto; José Ferreira; Jorge Valentim; Joaquim Mateus Neto; Maria Amorim Morais

The first one occurred as we picked up people in Porto: the story of the disappointed girl with three suitcases.

Jacques: "One of the girls had to be picked up at a pre-determined venue, a railroad station. She stood there on the sidewalk outside one of the Porto suburban platforms, keeping an eye out for us–with three suitcases next to her and elegantly dressed in sharp high heeled dress shoes. I made her break off her heels (no fooling!) and told her to leave the three suitcases on the station platform…"

Chuck: "Those suitcases are probably still gathering dust in some corner of the Lost and Found station depot …This was part of the agenda. We were all afraid. We did not know if the *PIDE* had an alert out for us (it was easy to spot Africans and Americans, after all…) and we had to get moving in our crowded automobiles!"

The second, on June 23rd– a close call on the way to Braga with "Iko" Carrera

Jacques: "I was to pick up Henrique Carreira in my car. He was in Porto. It was the day of the *Festa de Sao Joao,* 23rd June. He was a military officer, the only one in the group, and had with him–as we later found out–his service revolver. I went to pick him up at the appointed place. We had calculated that Saturday, June 24th, was the most propitious day for him to be on leave since Sunday, June 25th, was a day off for him at the Portuguese Army barracks and Monday the 26th being another local holiday. There was a good chance, therefore, that the military brass would not wake up to a new case of AWOL among its officers until Tuesday morning."

Jacques continues: "So, I was driving this automobile with three of our chaps inside, including Carreira. (Chuck was in another car in front of us with four others.) The back road which we had chosen to drive north was narrow, sinewy and hemmed in on both sides by deep ditches, quite dark and hard to see. Suddenly in a moment of inattention I ran off the road and into the right ditch–full of water! Just then a civil policeman rode by on his motor scooter and took me riding on the back seat to the nearest garage whose owner promptly came to pull us out of the ditch. The three guys who had stayed behind in the car – including the deserter Carreira–stayed quietly where they were all that time, but our bicycling policeman manifested no curiosity whatever !"

On June 23rd, at midnight through Braga, we had a third scare

Chuck: "Jacques was driving behind me. We were entering the city of Braga, where we emerged from a long midnight ride into a hugely lit main square full of hundreds of citizens celebrating the *Festa de São João* (The Feast of St. John's Eve) which Jacques had mentioned above. It was just after midnight. Our two automobiles crawled at a snail's pace through the crowds. It was scary because several excitable, slightly drunk, men crowded around our slow-moving vehicles after spying our African guests inside, gleefully shouting "*Pelé! Pelé!*", the Black Brazilian soccer star. At that moment we thought, this is it for sure, the cops will come and check it out. However, another miracle, they didn't. Probably any policemen would be off duty in any case, this being the most celebrated traditional popular feast of the year in Portugal, with the entire population out in the streets and square, eating at street food stalls, following processions, dancing in street festivals, sending hot air balloons up into the sky and– after midnight, watching spectacular fireworks above the town. It was about then when we popped into town and entered the packed main square. I was thinking– well, so much for precise amateur planning! On hindsight, wasn't it a brilliant idea to divert attention from our 2-car caravan ?"

June 24th just after midnight: A fourth critical moment– the aborted delivery

Chuck: "That same night as I drove my large black Plymouth we were headed for the planned rendezvous with one of the smuggler's sons, just this side of the Portuguese/Spanish border. After the crowds in the main square in Braga we started relaxing but started to look carefully for the turn-off to the right on the narrow road from Monção to Melgaço, which ran parallel to the Minho River. It was about 2 a.m. I anticipated seeing the smuggler's envoy along the side of the road."

"What we were not aware of, however, is that a message had been sent at the last minute by the smuggler destined for us through his contact in Lisbon. He was to pass it on to us at the hotel where we were staying in Porto. The message was, in a nutshell: 'Don't come tonight. The coast is not clear along the border. There's suspicious border guard activity.

We should lay low and postpone the trip. We will call later when things are safe."

"The trouble was, we never received the message. When we approached the place along the road next to a clump of bushes where he would be hiding, he was to step out from behind the bushes at precisely 2 am, as our cars arrived. When we drove slowly by the appointed spot, no smuggler. Nobody stepped out from behind the bushes! We waited for half an hour. Our Africans got out of the car and hid even further back underneath some pine trees. At that point we then decided that only one car, driven by Jacques, would return to Porto with its load. It could not take all eight persons, so four remained in the woods. I parked the car I was driving elsewhere, hidden from view, and set out to look for the house of one of the smuggler's cousins in the village. By then it was about 3 am and dawn would be up in a couple of hours. It was also very risky because I had only a vague notion of the village layout. There was a full, bright moon. It was nuts. Later, I thought: here I was headed for a village, totally unfamiliar to me and where every dog in northern Portugal began to bark wildly at the sight of a white-suited walker down pebble-strewn paths– surely a warning sign for border guards a couple of kilometres away. But what else could I do? (thought I). By sheer luck and the amused guidance of an insomniac neighbor smoking a cigarette in front of his door, I found the house and knocked. Our smuggler contact, astonished at seeing me through his screen door, then informed me about the message which had been sent earlier to us. Promptly he accompanied me back to the car–shushing every dog along the way–and sent us off, greatly relieved, on our two-hour drive back to Porto, to join Jacques and wait for the next night's adventure on Sunday the 25th."

Chuck continues: "You have to imagine how it was during those two weeks: we were taking decisions so fast and had to act so rapidly that it is hard now to account for the minute by minute story. We were under tremendous pressure to get these people out of Portugal, across Spain and into France before the Portuguese secret police, the PIDE, woke up!"

A fifth hair–raising incident

Chuck: "Carreira had been in our group of eight. We were forced to return to Porto from the border. He switched to my car in the woods and Jacques took off with four others. When we returned to Porto it was already dawn when we had entered the outskirts of the city. The fog was dense. I was driving at high speed and–too late–suddenly saw a roundabout intersection looming in front of us. The front wheels hit the curb hard. One tire burst. And there was Carreira our AWOL officer sitting in the back of the car!"

Jacques: "With his American-issue service revolver under his armpit".

Carreira was then a captain in the Portuguese army base in Porto. To avoid having to be shipped to Angola and thus be forced to fight his own countrymen, he had simply deserted– with his service revolver intact–and climbed into one of the automobiles headed for the *Rio Minho*. (For the record, "Iko" Carreira later became a legendary hero of independence in Angola, and appointed the Minister of Defense in its first government).

Bill, getting ahead of the story, adds: "…which is why the officer at the Spanish jail–with the last group of Africans under arrest–was more than happy to pick up the American-manufactured revolver and discretely place it without a word into his desk drawer!"

Chuck: …"There we were heading for disaster again, since on the other side of the misty roundabout two sleepy policemen sat parked in their cruiser … and actually came out to give us a hand to change the tire, pretty much ignoring the passengers carefully standing at an opaque, foggy distance away until the job was done. Fortunately, all eight of our passengers were able to hide out with friends throughout the long Sunday, until Jacques and I picked them up for the trip to the Minho River again. This time our smuggler friend was there by the bushes at 2 am, with fresh (smuggled, no doubt) batteries in his pin-point flashlight. His smile was brighter than the moon, and so were ours."

L. to R.: in the second group of 41: Henrique Carreira, Hilda Carreira, Kim Jones, Zacarias Cardoso, João Jamisse Nhambo, Armando Augusto Fortes, Fernando Paiva; Crouching in front: Joaquim Chissano, Henrique Santos de Carvalho, Fernando Chaves.

June 25th: meeting at the barn

Bill: "Meanwhile, we had received the *mots d'ordre v*ia Chuck that there would be a new group of eight Africans waiting for us at the barn. I split up the guys and directed them into each of the two autos driven by Kim and David, with instructions to them that they should deposit them at the home of Pastor Daniel Vidal, in San Sebastian, and then to return to Pontevedra right away!"

Chuck had meanwhile warned Bill that there would be a 24-hour delay in "delivery", and that they would be hiding in the barn on Sunday morning the 25th.

June 25th, a Sunday: 13h00 on the Galicia side of the border

Bill was there waiting. He then made sure that the papers were sorted out with the three American drivers, Dave,

Dick and Kim. After an 800 mile trip from San Sebastian to Pontevedra (and a welcome night's rest), the three American students and Bill drove up to the isolated predetermined point just inside the Spanish border in Galicia. The familiar barn was there by the dusty road, still large and rather abandoned-looking, still very dark inside–located at the top of a steep hill up from the *Minho* River. The cluster of men and women which had crossed by boat before dawn was there.

Bill narrates: "Our drivers re-grouped in Pontevedra. We had more signals from Chuck, made another run to the border and sent a group with two cars to San Sebastien. I stood on a corner and gave a note to the driver to leave them at the parsonage and return directly. Others were placed with the smuggler's family, and a third trip to the border took place a few days later. Each time, Edward G. came up with the ultimate plan and then had to think up something better. Also, the price went up. On the last night, a rumor was spread that 200 kilos of coffee were coming across the border. Police were beating the bushes all night, were worn out the following morning, and we went after our guys at siesta time.

June 25: Bill and Dick fetch more at the barn to put them up at the smuggler's home

Bill: "Dick and I in the meantime went to fetch the third group (*le troisième volet*) at the border barn. Jacques had told us that we should not travel immediately to San Sebastian but that we should take this third group to the nearby house of the smuggler in Arcade–with whom, I suppose, Jacques had worked out some deal. We did just that. At that point we received information from Portugal that there would be a fourth "package" about ready to cross over.

"We found we had a total of forty one Africans on our hands, more than our four automobiles could carry. In addition, the wear and tear of potholes and unremitting driving had caused last-minute breakdowns of two of the cars in Galicia, so I decided to negotiate a rental contract with the owner of a picturesque provincial bus and asked

Dick Wiborg to be the tour guide of a 'group of pilgrims.' Dick was given my hat to look more mature and was made the leader of *Gran Turismo*.

Chuck said later: "So that was how, to the amusement of some of the Angolan passengers, they became religious tourists."

Dick Wiborg narrates: "We rented an old Dodge bus and took a "tour" across northern Spain. Bill stayed behind in Pontevedra. So, on Monday morning the 26th I started off with a local village Spanish driver and a busload of Angolans, these "devout pilgrims," to visit, among other places, St. Jacques de Compostella. Our group included José Vieira Lopes, his wife Virginia and their son Johnny (*Djoni*). We travelled the entire way across northern Spain to San Sebastian. Exhausted, the Africans were soon invited to join Dave and Kim's groups in the top floor of Pastor Vidal's parsonage."

It was the San Sebastian parish of the Spanish Evangelical Church. Under very tense circumstances Vidal and his wife kept these carloads of African "guests" for several days and nights fed and lodged– unseen and unheard (with children!) from both church visitors and sidewalk passersby. Vidal and his wife's health later paid a heavy personal price for that courageous solidarity.

All forty-one in the second group had arrived in San Sebastien by Thursday night June 29th, including a small child and a very pregnant woman. (She and her husband were carrying false papers identifying them, coincidentally, as "Mary" and "Joseph"!) Back in Pontevedra, Dick's rented car, left behind in favor of the bus, was picked up by Chuck Harper and driven to San Sebastien with Jacques in the passenger seat and finally, after an emergency detour to Madrid–more later on that story–to Hendaye and delivered to the Hertz agency in Bayonne.

The bus

Bill and his three drivers, exhausted, booked into a San Sebastian hotel, wondering how in the world they would transport everyone across the border to France. They had already paid off the Pontevedra bus driver. Then they spied him walking across the *plaza* about to take off and ran down to sign him on again to take some of the charges across the border into France.

Bill recalls that after those days he never saw Daniel Vidal again until the World Council of Churches Conference at El Escorial in 1987, where they recalled the incidents. But it was Canberra, 1991, when Chuck Harper, Dave Pomeroy and Bill sat with Vidal to really reminisce. He told them what a strain it had been to put up a bunch of students in the attic, preparing meals, providing beds and keeping them quiet, especially the children. It was particularly tough on his wife, who miscarried a few weeks later. To add to the tension, during the African presence upstairs, a church *consistoire* was meeting in the parsonage. He told his fellow pastors: "If you see anything strange, you must not ask any questions!" During their meeting, their eyes would widen as one or another male or female student would tip-toe to the bathroom, but they kept it all to themselves. Their training in discretion was based on decades of distrust and harassing suffered by Protestants under the Franco regime. Pastor Daniel died in 1994.

7

The prison

An incident which could have had catastrophic consequences almost plunged the operation into total disaster: the last group which arrived in the bus with Dick, joining those who were waiting in Pastor Vidal's parish house, was suddenly detained by the Spanish police on Friday the 30th of June. Suspicious border police–one of whom had been reprimanded and fired by their superiors, it was learned later, for having allowed the first group of "disguised Portuguese Africans" out of the country–took no chances this time and made the cars turn around for a thorough check of identities at the main police station in San Sebastian. Each was interrogated. All, under pressure, revealed their identities and showed not only their false passports but also the covering documents issued by CIMADE guaranteeing them safe haven in France.

At that point, the real threat of a forced repatriation to Portugal weighed very heavily on their spirits. As a pastor and the senior CIMADE member in the Spanish team, Bill had to negotiate their permission to cross the border into France, but to no avail. They were all formally arrested and jailed.

Bill: "It was the patron saint's day at Irun, so everyone was wearing white shirts and red berets, getting ready for the parade which was coming soon. Arriving at the government office, I went in with all our papers. The man in charge–different from the last time–waved the papers in my face and said, "Are these the Angolans you are sneaking into

France?" I said, "Monsieur, all I know is that the papers they are carrying are from an embassy in Paris, not made up by amateurs or crooks." I went on to say we counted on his *compréhension* not his *credulité*. He said the other man had had a lot of trouble, but I think he was bluffing."

"He settled down, said he had to have the authorization of the governor's representative just as a formality, and for us to meet him at 4:00 p.m. at a given address. We sat for hours in our cars and bus, watched the parade, and tried to keep cool. I tore up the part of the map showing the border crossing point and prayed everything would turn out alright."

"At 4 o'clock, we drove up to a pleasant looking building–more like a residence with lawn and trees and flowers. As soon as we got parked, a dozen policemen surrounded our cars, told us to bring our belongings to the house. I knew we had been trapped. The long delay had been due to rounding up officers on their holiday!"

"I was ushered into an office, where an older man sat behind the desk, and an interrogation began by a detective in a flowery sport shirt. He became known to us as 'Jean Gabin,', the popular French actor, whom he resembled. We spoke French, since I had no Spanish and they no English. They asked about all this and as they were coming up with the CIMADE political asylum identity papers, I told them the story of humanitarian concern which brought us there and that I was a Protestant minister and that CIMADE was an ecumenical service organization. They shook their heads and said, *"Político, político."* I did not mention where we picked up our friends or who had helped us, and they didn't ask"

"Finally, 'Jean Gabin' typed up his report and paused to confirm in his own words: *Monsieur le pasteur, vous avez fait ça par obéissance religieuse, n'est-ce pas?* ("Pastor, you did that by religious obedience, right?") I said very sincerely, "Oui, Monsieur, merci." It was a Catholic expression I really appreciated!"

"At one point, a detective came to the door and asked me to give him a hand with one of the girl students who was refusing to turn over her CIMADE identification. I assured her it was O.K. since it was the real identity the police insisted on having before letting us go on across the border. With some of them, there was obviously strict discipline. Another student told me he had eaten his! A second time, an Angolan called me to the door to say they were going to find a pistol in his bag. I said, "What did you bring a pistol for?" His answer was an unbelieving: "It was *my* pistol!" I went with another officer to find the bag and told him that my friend had not known what to expect on this trip and had been so 'foolish as to bring his Portuguese army gun'. The detective scoffed at that until he pulled it out, saying, "It's a pistol!" I yelled, "I told you so." (This Angolan was Iko Carreira, later Minister of Defense for the MPLA government. He once told Jacques Beaumont that his Portuguese officer's pistol was of U.S. manufacture and had been provided through NATO. Ironically, the same kinds of weapons were provided later by the US to UNITA during the civil war in independent Angola, against his own army!)"

"We went back into the office–which I remember more as a living room–where I explained to the boss what had happened. He brushed it off, put the pistol in a drawer of his desk, and that was the end of it. I didn't get upset until I saw them taking our guys out in hand-cuffs. 'Jean Gabin' said we were just being put up overnight at the provincial prison 'because the hotels were full this time of year.' Oh, sure! My fear was that Dave, Kim and I would be put somewhere better than the others, and I didn't want that. Mysteriously, Dick had not been taken in and remained at the border bridge wondering what had become of us!"

"The police took us to the prison jail. We were stripped, searched, then led into a large room where all the men students were put– probably about 35. The women and little Johnny were somewhere else, I think in separate cells. The women were frisked in a separate room by female agents. Then the money and personal belongings of each one of us were carefully registered. You should have seen their eyes bulge when they saw how much money I had on me for the operation! There were several million pesetas–to cover costs of hotels, restaurants, car rentals–for the 41 and ourselves. After the searches we were all told to gather in a large room. I was very glad that we were finally all back together again and not separated. One agent explained to me that they had earlier handcuffed the Africans to keep someone from panicking or from 'doing something stupid' like running... Clearly the prison rooms and cells had to be cleaned up and prepared to accommodate this large group. It was very late. We tried to sleep. I lay beside João Vieira, the leader of the 'political' group. Later on the MPLA guys stuck together, while the 'Protestants' each made their own plans. Somehow Vieira kept the funds for the group even through the search. There were soiled mattresses on the floor, on which we spent the night."

"On Saturday morning, July 1st, in the early dawn as people started waking up, we tried to raise morale by singing. It started with a prayer session which I began. Then we sang 'We Shall Overcome'. Someone had a piece of paper which he scraped in rhythm on the cement floor, as accompaniment. But then the guards brought in folding metal cots in the early morning and put our mattresses on them. I began to get very apprehensive–it looked as if we were going to stay there for a while."

Dave remembers: "This was a very low moment throughout this Saturday. The Angolans sang some songs and tried to get some sleep. But we all were thinking about the possible repercussions if we were sent back to Portugal : the possibility that the three of us might be tried for kidnapping; the fact that the Army deserters could well be shot; the fact that most of the Angolans would probably end up in prison. These were not pleasant thoughts to occupy us."

Bill: "Saturday morning everybody was pretty glum. I tried to keep their morale up, talking about friends in Paris and even Washington and Adlai Stephenson's speech at the U.N. calling for Angolan independence. At the suggestion of the students, I wrote a letter to the American consul in Bilbao, including a statement signed by all the prisoners in their right names. They asked for the protection of the United States in the cause of human rights. In retrospect, we suppose the letter was never delivered.

Jacques: "You probably gave this letter to the prison administrator. You don't have the proof that he delivered it, so we cannot say that the consul in Bilbao did nothing, right?" Bill: "I agree. Except that when I wrote to him later asking about the letter he did not express any interest in what I wrote and asked no questions." Jacques: "The prison director could very well have transmitted the letter to the consul, either in Madrid or in Bilbao, or could have kept it himself. He might have wished to avoid another international incident, saying to himself 'Let's get rid of the problem… above all on a holiday, the jour de Fête!'. Therefore, we don't really have proof that the American consul in Bilbao did receive the letter from you." Jacques: "Consulates and embassies are full of people who are frightened of being declared *persona non grata*. The chap–it was understandable– simply did not wish to dig deeper into what was, after all, illegal and a possible scandal."

About noon, a member of the group was taken out for questioning. We waited. After all, it was a holiday week-end, so how could the police do anything? I showed everybody the flamenco doll I had bought for our daughter Doe, and we talked about our families. One of the guys talked about the trip through the woods, the boat, hiding in the cornfield and said, "It was just like in the movies." A stereotype of Africa was dislodged also when one of them said the only wild animals he'd ever seen were in a zoo.

Inside the prison with José Vieira Lopes and little Djoni

Bill: "After a time, our friend returned, jubilant that we were going to be released. Everyone rejoiced, but I was suspicious and said to myself, 'It's another trick.' But sure enough, the instructions came to 'get ready to leave'." One of the prisoners later said: "On the second day of our detention– this was on July 2nd–the director of the establishment came into our prison unannounced. What was our astonishment when he started to express his appreciation and that of the people and government of Spain, for all those, around the world, who were fighting for freedom and independence. In addition he apologized for the inconvenience caused by our detention and announced that we were to be driven to the border with France, where political asylum was guaranteed. What we certainly did not expect was to hear words of an official sympathetic to the Third World, speaking like a leftist. This coming from the mouth of a representative of a repressive apparatus of the Franco regime! The one who was mostly unconvinced by this statement was the Angolan Methodist pastor who continued to wish us courage as we faced the inevitable firing squad."

Bill: "They issued us our belongings and out we went to get our cars and bus. Maybe it was a police bus this time. 'Jean Gabin' said, 'I told you so.' He took me in for a drink at a cafe and said, 'You've got to come back to San Sebastian. It's a great tourist town.' We had lost a small souvenir Toledo pen-knife which he helped me look for, but it disappeared between incarceration and release.

Dave reports: "Then about five PM in the afternoon, I was asleep and Bill woke me up and said, 'We're getting out. I don't know if it's good or bad, but we're getting out.' At 6h30 pm, they started moving us. We went through the same procedure, with a thorough search, fingerprinting again…

We got back all our personal possessions—or most of them. It was a long, red-taped procedure. It wasn't until 9 pm that we were all back at the Governor's place in San Sebastian… So the police commissioner takes us back to the border".

Chuck adds: "Suddenly, in the late afternoon their Basque jailers, supposedly under orders from Madrid, informed them that they would be released. There was at first incomprehension, then suspicion–and finally deep relief. The formal procedures were repeated, in reverse. All were taken in vehicles to the border, driven across and left to disembark in front of the French border *douane* (customs)."

8

Freedom at last–crossing into France

Bill continues: "As we approached the French side of the bridge on Saturday night, I jumped out with all our papers. The agent in traditional *kepi* (cap) of the French police called his chief at home and said, 'It's too late to process this, go back to Spain for the night!'

I said, 'Nothing doing!. We'll spend the night here if we have to.' Explaining we had authorization from Paris, I got him to let me and Dave Pomeroy go into Hendaye and phone CIMADE. Of course, our American passports were O.K."

Tania Metzel

"As we entered the hotel we had used before, I made straight for the desk. The clerk said, 'Just a minute, we're making a call,' and the next moment said into the speaker, *Solferino 93-99?* I jumped and said, 'That's CIMADE. Who's calling?' He said a lady in Room 10 who had just arrived. I burst into the room and found Tania Metzel. Because she was the official Prisons chaplain, representing the Protestant Federation of France, she could guess what had happened. She told Madeleine Barot and others when we dropped out of sight that we had to be in the provincial prison, because nowhere else could accommodate our 41 students plus American drivers. Dave remembered that when she saw us, she said in typical Tania style: 'I expected much, but not so much!'"

"She accompanied us to the bridge, convinced the agent that she would bring the group back on Sunday morning, and on the strength of her own chaplain credentials took responsibility for the students. At the border Saturday night, the role of Tania Metzel waiting on the other side turned out to be a crucial one. She had just come from Paris. The French border guard was extremely reticent to let these people through. He was all alone on this Saturday evening. Metzel's important official position as a French national civil servant, her imposing natural authority and vigorous personality overcame any hesitation which the agent could have harbored in taking such a momentous decision by himself. It combined with the assurances which the Ministry of the Interior communicated to the border police, granting a *laissez-passer* to the forty-one Africans. Kim, Dave and I had to leave our passports at the post overnight, which is how the right-wing newspaper *La Nation Française* got our names to print an article later on. We got into the hotel and settled down, still not believing our good fortune."

Bill: "Sunday after breakfast, we went back to the border–I suppose this meant a lot of taxis, but I don't remember–and Tania helped the customs agents and border police to verify identities."

Jacques: "I believe that at a key moment on Sunday morning when the group returned to the French police checkpoint on the bridge, a government ministry in Paris telephoned to the *Préfecture de Bayonne* (police headquarters in Bayonne), because this prefecture is mentioned in the article referred to above. We can only assume that it was the Ministry of Foreign Affairs or the Ministry of the Interior which made the call. Which one? A mystery! We do know that a call was made–and the information was passed on to border agents in Hendaye–confirming the authenticity of the signature of Pastor Marc Boegner–President of CIMADE–a signature which was on the CIMADE documents in the possession of each of the members of the African group."

Bill: "It is also possible that Tania made a direct phone call in the presence of the police officer to someone in the government. After Tania had helped the police to identify all these students she came out of the building. One of the students then asked her 'Well, what happens now?' To which Tania replied: '*Rien! Vous êtes libres*'! ('Nothing! You are free.')

"There was a second of total silence and astonishment, then a tremendous shouting and embracing. We had done it! As I told Chuck later, my remark to one of the students was: 'I think God must have really wanted you out of Portugal!' I said to Dick, Dave, and Kim: 'Makes you believe in the Red Sea, doesn't it?'

Free at last, outside the French border post at Hendaye, L. to R. : Africano Neto, Henrique Santos de Carvalho, Tomas Medeiros, José Carlos Antonette, Carlos Pestana Heineken, Joaquim Chissano, Fernando Chaves. In the background: Tania Metzel and Pedro Filipe.

"They had benefited in great part from a discreet intervention from Paris, alerted as it had been by various persons in Spain and by CIMADE. Whether the Kennedy administration was informed, as some have claimed, of the detention overnight of an 'élite' group of future African leaders, or not, the material evidence of such an intervention has not yet been forthcoming".

According to documents contained in the archives of the former PIDE, the Prime Minister of Portugal, Antonio Salazar, had even dispatched a plane from Lisbon to San Sebastian to retrieve the group, but his request was denied by the Spanish authorities, clearly forestalling an international outcry and the inevitable damage to Spain's image. One can only imagine Salazar's fury.

Back at the hotel, the group had a feast with speeches and tributes and singing. Lots of prayers of thanksgiving and praise. In the midst of all this celebration, in walk Chuck and Jacques, having driven from Madrid. '*Hurra!*','*Viva!*' So much had happened since we had picked them up on some corner in Portugal and now had joined them again in France!

A detour to Madrid the night before

Jacques and Chuck had driven Dick's car to San Sebastian, then found out from Daniel Vidal that the group had been arrested, and immediately drove to Madrid for help. It took six high-speed hours to get there. Around midnight they rang the bell at the apartment of a high official in the Foreign Office of the Spanish government who was a member of the Protestant church. It was only after they had spent a half-hour telling him what was happening that he finally revealed that he had just received a telegram that the students had been released. He was holding it in his hand when he had opened the door!

Outside the hotel restaurant in Hendaye where all celebrated their freedom–Left to right: Maria de Luz Boal; Manuel Boal; Mimosa Rodriguez; José Araújo; Joaquim Chissano; Augusto Lopes Teixeira; Mário Clington; Dick Wiborg; Xavier Belém Rodrigues; Bill Nottingham; Maria Ilda Carreira; Margarida Mangueira Van Dunem; Ana Wilson; Augusto Wilson; Zacariias Cardoso; Fernando Paiva; Teresa Pedro Gomes

A call for unity

At the Sunday meal Jacques made an unforgettable speech to our group of African students: "*Stay united!*. Do not let political division ruin your struggle." He knew that the rival political movements would be hard to reconcile. The first stirrings of rebellion in Angola had been felt with the founding, in 1954, of *NAPU* (*União das Populações do Norte da Angola*), a movement led by Holden Roberto in northern Angola. This political organization widened its constituency to become known, in 1961, as the *UPA* (*União dos Povos Angolanos*). A year later it joined another small group of nationalists (the *PDA–O Partido Democrático de Angola*) from Congo-Léopoldville (later Kinshasa) to become the *FNLA*, the *Frente Nacional de Libertação de Angola*, still under the leadership of Roberto. From its base in the Congo, the *FNLA* received considerable assistance from the organization of African Unity, the People's Republic of China and the United States of America.

The *MPLA* (*Movimento Popular de Libertação de Angola*) was founded in the 1950s, but it suffered heavy losses among its first militants. In 1962 it was re-grouped by Agostinho Neto, a Mbundu physician who spent several years in an Angolan prison but subsequently escaped to Portugal. After a short period in Congo-Kinshasa, Neto transferred the headquarters of the *MPLA* to Congo-Brazzaville, and later, in 1965, to Zambia, taking advantage of more direct access to the populations in neighboring Angola. By 1965, the rivalries between these two main rival movements, the *FLNA* and the *MPLA*, constituted a serious obstacle to achieving national independence and the requisite international backing for it. In 1966 a third nationalist force appeared–*UNITA* (*União Nacional Para a Independência Total de Angola*), with leaders mainly from the Angolan Ovimbundu ethnic group. *UNITA* was led by Jonas Savimbi, a former minister of external affairs of the *FLNA*. After leaving the *FLNA* in 1964, Savimbi went to mainland China where he received military training and was strongly influenced by Maoism.

Bill: "I often thought of that, as the war of independence from Portugal waged on for more than a decade and then ideological civil wars until the death of Savimbi in 2002, with no end in sight yet for Angola."

"We returned the cars–mud-spattered and with thousands of kilometers racked up. The boss's wife was furious, but we paid up well and left on the train with our friends. The logistics of all this were impressive. Just our part of it cost the Methodists $50,000 with more still to come."

"We learned later that Dick and Dave thought it would be fun to go back on their own to that restaurant at Bidart near Biarritz, to see the friendly waitress Roseanne again. I think she wasn't there but the guys did decide to go swimming. They knew nothing about the surf and tides in the Bay of Biscay. When they had swum awhile, they found they were a little further out than they intended and they started back. But the harder they swam the further they were from the beach! Their cries were heard by someone who swam out to them with a rope secured on shore and they hauled themselves in. We later spoke about this narrowly averted tragedy and how we would have attributed it, for the record, to something sinister, related to our liberation of the Angolans."

"The anti-climax came upon arrival in Paris. Someone had not been clear about the buses, so we stood around a long time before they came. Jacques was in a rage. Patti met me. I presented some of our friends. She had Japanese-American Disciple fraternal workers with her on a visit from Germany. We were all very tense, and I insisted on the need for security to protect friends in Spain and Portugal. Pat had been through a lot waiting for the outcome since I had left. She had had phlebitis from a bump on her leg, running after the kids without me, but when Madeleine phoned on the previous Saturday to ask if she had heard from me, it cured itself! Madeleine said we were either in jail or had driven off the road into the sea. We never understood whether or not she was being facetious. But everything I did was part of Pat's commitment also. We would take pride 30 years later that so many of the students had become leaders in the governments of five African countries and that among the students in jail with us were Joaquim Chissano and

Pascual Macumbi–future president and foreign minister of Mozambique and Pedro Pires, future president of Cape Verde".

In Paris, a turn of events: a visit from Edouardo Mondlane, Mozambique's independence leader

Bill: "As time went on, we saw the students at Sèvres and had a few of the Protestants for dinner in our apartment. Things became slow and frustrating for them. One day, I was asked to go to Orly and pick up Dr. Edouardo Mondlane from the U.S.A. who wanted to meet the students from Mozambique. This tall, handsome man was a professor at Syracuse University with a Ph.D. in sociology. He was also from a family of chiefs in Mozambique and a member of Congregational background–now the United Church of Christ. Later, United Church of Christ missionaries Ed and Gretchen Hawley would be attached to his headquarters in Dar-es-Salaam! Eduardo told me that Robert Service of the U.S. State Department had gotten in touch with him. John Kennedy himself saw a cable from the embassy in Bern that 19 Angolans had been received in Switzerland and sent Mr. Service to check it out and see that they were offered scholarships to study in the U.S.A. There had been a glitch in Paris, where this first bunch were only allowed to stay two weeks. Jacques had to return from Lisbon to handle it and to protest for the next group."

"Dr. Mondlane could hardly fold his large frame in my little Renault 4 CV, but I got him to Sèvres. There were six or seven Mozambicans, I believe, but they became the nucleus of the liberation movement *FRELIMO*, which Mondlane organized or was in the process of organizing. In a few years he was actually leading a guerilla group in Mozambique–a colony of Portugal the size of California since the time of the 15th century Portuguese navigator Vasco da Gama. Mozambique was rich in resources and naturally beautiful, with superb beaches and commercial ports on the Indian Ocean."

"I met Dr. Mondlane again in the apartment of Mia Adjali in New York that fall and near Philadelphia in a retreat center with our African friends in December with Gary Oniki, United Church of Christ executive for Africa. Edouardo was a very impressive person, a Christian married to an American whom he had met in Oberlin as a student. Ed Hawley was university chaplain and officiated at their wedding. Edouardo was a man of destiny fitted to guide an independent Mozambique in a democratic direction during the competitive pressures of the Cold War. He was killed in February 1969 by a letter bomb in his office in Dar-es-Salaam. I got the word at a meeting of the UCC somewhere, Chicago I think. It was a fatal blow to Mozambican unity, probably caused by former Portuguese settlers, Rhodesian whites under Ian Smith, and right-wing South Africans backing *RENAMO*. But I also heard that a traitor in *FRELIMO* named Dlhakama was involved. He became a negotiator later with the *RENAMO* rebels after 17 years of civil war, following the war of independence from Portugal which lasted into the 1970's. Samora Machel succeeded Edouardo, played the Soviet Union card, and alienated the U.S. He was killed in a plane crash in the 1980's, and Joaquin Chissano, one of our Fuga students, became president. A tentative peace came in 1990 or 1991. Miriam Wells, U.S. ambassador, helped restore U.S. relations and sympathies."

"I'll tell the story of Samora Machel and Sir Garfield Todd later! My visit to Mozambique in October, 1990, is also another story, with an invitation by Pascoal Macumbi and Chissano, but the political turmoil prevented my seeing the president at the last minute."

"The famous Portuguese secret police PIDE never got wind of these sixty escapees until the Spanish police told them. As a result of this 'pilgrimage to St. Jacques,' Mali was the first African nation to break diplomatic relations with Portugal, soon to be followed by nearly all the rest except South Africa and Rhodesia. Years later, in September 1993, President Chissano told a group in New York about his country's friendship with America and about being in jail in Spain with people who had helped the struggle of his people. I know he considers it important to remember that this was an action of the churches!"

The CIMADE backup team in Paris

Jacques: "It took several of us considerable effort to obtain scholarships in Switzerland. It was Véronique Laufer– herself a Swiss citizen- who played a key role here. Besides having 'sat by the phone' at the CIMADE headquarters day and night during the two weeks in June when we were carrying out the operation, it was she who obtained visas from the Swiss Ambassador in Paris, quite exceptionally, so that several students might study there (with scholarships provided by the Swiss churches). It was a miracle!"

Véronique Laufer was a member of the General Secretariat of CIMADE in 1961 and thus a close associate of both Jacques Beaumont and Bill Nottingham. Immediately following the decisions taken by the WCC and the CIMADE leadership in Leysin, Switzerland, to launch the clandestine operation, Véronique became fully involved in its planning and execution during June and early July. In her written narrative, she notes that "for a whole month I didn't leave the Rue de Grenelle headquarters of CIMADE, night or day." She was quite literally waiting by the phone for instructions from Jacques, the single senior member of the staff responsible for any emergencies.

Two instances–among others–stand out in which her action was indispensable for the success of the operation. One was when she stayed up all night in a small back office of the Senegalese embassy, standing next to the consul who "typed with two fingers on an old typewriter" fictitious but plausible Senegalese names, birthplaces and professions onto official *titres de voyage* ("safe-passage documents"). Meanwhile she dictated to him authentic addresses from the pages of African immigrant neighborhoods of the Paris phone book...."That", she wrote, "is how one Angolan became a Senegalese pearl diver, or another a shoemaker". And it worked for the first nineteen who crossed the border into France!

Another time was when she received an urgent telephone call on June 19th from Pastor Marc Boegner, saying that he had been contacted by the French Foreign Ministry by a certain "Monsieur Simon". This latter wished to know why those first nineteen Angolan and other Portuguese colonials were trying to enter France with CIMADE documents, signed by Boegner, guaranteeing responsibility for their stay and *prise en charge* ("living expenses"). "He told me to go to the Foreign Office immediately and to explain the situation. This I did for an hour, telling this civil servant–whose plaque on the door indicated that he was responsible for the "Iberian Peninsula"–all we knew about the situation affecting these students under the Salazar regime, the forced labor of Angolans in South African gold mines, the forced recruitment into the Army, the studies they were accomplishing in Lisbon, Coimbra, and Porto under precarious conditions and the constant harassment by the Portuguese political police, the *PIDE*…, even leading some to be arrested and sometimes tortured". Talks had taken place between Boegner and the Minister of Foreign Affairs, Maurice Couve de Murville, but the Minister was not in the city when the nineteen arrived at the border. This effective briefing greatly helped to speed the authorization for the nineteen Angolans to enter France, with their *sauf-conduits de la Cimade* ("CIMADE safe passage papers"). Véronique Laufer concluded her term of service with CIMADE in 1962, at which time she returned to Switzerland and was assigned responsibilities with the WCC.

The flight of forty-three students to Germany and dispersal to fight or study.

Bill: "Time dragged on for the African young people in Paris. Pat and I were preparing to return to the United States in August, completing three years with CIMADE. Dick, Dave and Kim finished their summer and returned to New York. We had a final reunion at our apartment in Flatbush the following spring."

"However, before we left Paris, CIMADE was stunned by the departure of all of the MPLA Angolan students by bus for the German border with the connivance of the embassy of Ghana. From Germany, they were flown to Africa for an experience of a country which had achieved independence. They were disenchanted after a time. Some wound up

Freedom at last—crossing into France 85

in Algeria training for guerilla warfare. Others chose the U.S.A. when an American official in Ghana offered them scholarships. Others went to Czechoslovakia. A number stayed in Western Europe to study. The mulatto, Roman Catholic, Marxist-oriented, urban young people were highly disciplined and stuck together, related to the *MPLA* which came to power in Angola later. The Protestant, black students tended to support Holden Roberto, backed by the CIA and succeeded by Jonas Savimbi and *UNITA* who prolonged the agony of Angola up to the time I write this."

Jacques added: " All this tension among the students at Sèvres created a climate ripe for the arrival of a certain anti-colonialist French lawyer who showed up in my office to ask me 'What is going on?'. It turned out that he rushed to help the students, promising them scholarships which he could not deliver, while surreptitiously arranging for transport and papers for the students to enter the Federal Republic of Germany–their cover being that they were members of an African cultural group. The result is that–after several weeks–on Saturday August 19th , forty-three of the original group of 60 students suddenly disappeared and left Paris for places unknown, which turned out to be West Germany, as reported above. Three months later, six of them returned from Germany to CIMADE, asking Véronique Laufer for new scholarship aid!" Eventually all the Angolans–and a few other lusophones–divided up and attended a certain number of universities in Eastern and Western Europe and the People's Republic of China."

Meanwhile, Jacques received a moving postcard, written only five days after the group left Sèvres, from one of the Africans who travelled to Germany, José de Azevedo Lima. In it he referred to his imperative "need to go back to Africa" at an important moment in his life when he had to make a critical choice–in spite of his love for Portugal and for his wife whom he left there, as well as his cousin. Lima wrote, "You are truly a friend, acting above religious or political considerations. I embrace you, *amicalement!*".

Azevedo Lima was a significant leader of the group, having been the president of the Federation of African

Students in Portugal at the time of the operation. He later sought political asylum in Brazil, where, after the military *coup d'état* there in 1964, he was arrested and tortured in the notorious DOPS headquarters in São Paulo in the presence, it is reported, of Portuguese PIDE agents. Subsequently he made his way back to Angola.

Chuck: "Some made it to Switzerland, others to England. The Americans had offered scholarships to some more of this group. Two or three others made their way to Guinée Bissau, and one or two to Tanzania where *FRELIMO*, the Mozambican liberation headquarters-in-exile was temporarily located. Most of the Mozambicans, including two women, had remained in Paris in any case. Joachim Chissano and Pascoal Mocumbi were among them. These two went to Poitiers, in France, with scholarships to study medicine. There were other trained physicians–such as Methodist Silvio Almeida, who had come out at another time. Another doctor went to Algeria after independence, became an Algerian citizen and became the Dean of the Faculty of Medicine in Algiers. Of the group of forty-three which disappeared on August 19 from Paris, only ten men and women travelled to Ghana. But they were highly motivated and ready as they already were seasoned, trained militants. These are the ones who flew to Ghana (Kwame Nkruma was in power then, whose powerful call that "Africa Must Unite" attracted many intellectuals across the continent). Four or five died in combat, others in exile. Two of them in Jonas Savimbi's camp in Angola, one on the *MPLA* side. Some disappeared–dropped out of sight in the West, so to speak. Two got married in the USA."

Jacques: "Some students finally ended up in Moscow to study at the Patrice Lumumba University. At first they had a tough time there, interrogated by the Soviet police wanting to know who they were. It was perfectly clear to the authorities that the students had fled from Portugal with the help of a Christian ecclesiastical network (*une filière chrétienne et eclesiastique*) and with Americans to boot ! It is true that they made it to the German border, undetected, and, if my memory is good, they took a regional train in the Saar region to Bonn. There they found themselves in a very delicate situation. In Germany there was confusion. The group began to divide up. Some went to the USSR. Eight or ten made their way back to France and showed up at the CIMADE headquarters in Rue de Grenelle. I welcomed them with *Vous êtes toujours libres !* ("You are still free!") The rest, therefore, were scattered East and West, to study or to work."

9

The Aftermath–Press reports, new destinations and encounters

Aftermath 1 : The Portuguese government press release dated July 14, 1961 and other press reports

The Ministry of Internal Affairs announces that Portuguese authorities have learned that a secret organization is active in Portugal with the purpose of involving in subversive activities students from Overseas who are studying here. According to gathered intelligence, this organization has its headquarters in a European country and is called: 'Organization for the Protection of Third World Countries,' and it acts among students to lead them to believe in the hypothetical and future persecution by the government and population because of what is happening in Northern Angola.

Although the procedures used are very crude and reprehensible, the truth is that the organization has managed to provoke some disturbances among the young people, and it can be concretely affirmed that 41 students from Overseas secretly crossed the border in June with the aid of a Protestant pastor and 3 North American students. According to investigations which have been made, the group was headed for France, using false passports provided by an embassy in Paris of an African country.

Although it can be presumed that such clandestine activities will not find a response among many more students–which at this moment already have been warned of the true motives of the organization– it has been found useful to warn the public in general, and the students from Overseas in particular, of the criminal purposes behind these activities and false 'things' which they pretend to serve. (Unofficial translation.)

Several Portuguese and French newspaper articles appeared in 1961 highlighting the lusophone African operation. However, they carried incomplete or erroneous information, as can be seen below. Madeleine Barot, in a letter which she wrote to Bill Nottingham on July 25, 1961, referred to articles which appeared in Switzerland and in England. Bill also pointed out that "an article later appeared with the names of all those who had been detained in San Sebastian, listed in the context of a meeting held in Prague in October 1961, under the auspices of the International Union of Students, a Soviet-sponsored youth organization. One student, from Portugal, took the floor at that meeting…They were all surprised".

Most of these news reports had made reference to, or were based upon, the press release put out by the Portuguese government Minister of the Interior on July 14th. The fact that so few articles on the operation appeared elsewhere in the secular media (given the international implications of the operation for Portugal and its colonies, for France and for the USA in that the highest political authorities in each country were to some degree or other touched by or involved in its *déroulement* or aftermath)–is truly remarkable. To our knowledge no major media outlets in these countries picked up the story. As Bill Nottingham replied to Madeleine Barot on July 28th, *Tant mieux!* ("It's a good thing they didn't!")

La Nation Française, on August 9, 1961 published a major story on pages one and eight, severely criticizing both CIMADE's President Marc Boegner, and implicitly the French government, for allowing the students to enter France. This right-wing newspaper, quite pro-*Algérie française*, headlined its story *Le Chemin des écoliers d'Angola : vers Prague via Hendaye et la Suisse* ("The road of the Angolan students leading to Prague by way of Hendaye and Switzerland"). A first page editorial is directed against Pastor Boegner, expressing the newspaper's "grave" concern and "sadness" over the fact that this illustrious personality is identified with the "game" which the Protestant missionaries in Angola are playing with Marxist revolutionaries. Additionally, it holds that he is being influenced by the policies of President Kennedy–allowing the students to "learn their trades" under the Soviets. The story on page nine reproduces a facsimile of the CIMADE letter which each of the Africans had carried, assuring the beneficiary of CIMADE's full administrative and financial responsibility for the student, while he or she were in France. It also gives details of the forty-one persons who had been detained in San Sebastian, as well as the full names of the three American citizens Nottingham, Pomeroy and Jones, as well as the person who was at Hendaye waiting for them, Tania Metzel. [Wiborg is not mentioned, because he was not in prison with the others.] In effect, the editors of this paper accuse the French Protestants, CIMADE, its President Marc Boegner and Senegal–who provided passports–of working hand in hand with those who perpetrated the "massacres of Budapest".

Le Monde published a short entry in its edition of April 21, 1963, almost two years after the operation had been carried out, announcing the setting up, in Paris, of a "Committee for the Defense" of Lewin Vidal, a "Frenchman" arrested by the Portuguese PIDE and held incommunicado. Vidal was the *fondé de pouvoir* (power of attorney) of the bank *Crédit franco-portugais* (a branch of the Crédit Lyonnais) and former member of the Student Christian Movement in Paris. In effect, Lewin Vidal's name and his role in the operation was traced by the PIDE. He was detained on April 3, 1963, subject to nonstop interrogation and kept from sleeping. The charges by the government were that he was suspected of being in touch with "Portuguese and Angolan" students actively opposed to the Salazar regime. Vidal was accused by the authorities for having assisted and disseminated "propaganda" in favour of Angolese "terrorists". He was sentenced to four months in prison, *incommunicado*. One of the two lawyers who still had not had access to see him, was Maître Jean-Jacques de Felice, a great friend of CIMADE and notably active in the defense of jailed French conscientious objectors against the war in Algeria at the time. (One of them was Tony Orengo, an équipier of the CIMADE team at the Boulevard des Dames, in Marseille). Vidal's wife was granted protection inside the French Embassy in Lisbon.

This piece elicited an indignant response by the press spokesman at the Portuguese Embassy in Paris, published by *Le Monde* the next day, and in which he maintained that Vidal indeed had become involved with "Angolan terrorists", but that he was under no constraints nor was being held *incommunicado* while being detained by the police. The spokesman also insisted that Vidal's French consul could visit him–as well as could his wife–and denied that she had taken refuge in the French embassy.

A solidarity committee working for his defense and release was soon set up in Paris during 1963 and 1964. Its active secretary, Marie-Lise Roux, a cousin in the Beaumont family, had also been a resident at the Parisian Protestant student hostel on the Rue Vaugirard. The article is in *Le Monde* dated 21 April 1963, entitled *Un Français au Secret depuis Trois Semaines dans une Prison Portugaise* ("A Frenchman in Solitary for Three Weeks in a Portuguese Prison.")

Aftermath 2 : The future leadership of the independent Portuguese-speaking African countries

Years later, when various members of the original group of students were elected to high positions of leadership in their countries or named to head up government ministries, various published articles recorded their careers. Some became career military officers, like Henrique ("Iko") Teles Carreira, who was the Minister of Defence under Agostinho Neto in Angola from 1975 to 1980. Some became political leaders such as Joachim Alberto Chissano who was elected president of Mozambique in 1986. This latter's brilliant career is recounted in some detail in a story which appeared in an East African newspaper dated November 4, 1986, headlined "Chissano New Leader of Mozambique", in which it is mentioned that after one year of studying in Lisbon, "he left clandestinely for France, when he joined the liberation movement". Ten years later Newsweek (March 13, 1995) ran a story ("Lessons from Mozambique") highlighting the remarkable role of President Chissano in forging reconciliation, peace and prosperity to his country after a bitter civil war.

In October of 2007 Joaquim Chissano was named the winner of the "Mo Ibrahim Prize" for good governance and achievement in African leadership. The prize is worth US$ 5 million, the largest individual award ever granted for such distinguished accomplishments.

Aftermath 3: Significant personal encounters–Paul Evdokimov, Pascoal Mocumbi, Edouardo Mondlane…

Jacques: "Three years later Paul Evdokimov told me that he had had a conversation with one of the students before they left for Germany–and that he, Evdokimov, took a decision without consulting me at all, to say to them 'You are free to go!'. He told me this one evening when we were tired and had had a bit of vodka together…I wasn't as upset as Madeleine was, because I felt that indeed each one was free to make his or her decision, without making a judgment about the political orientations they had."

Bill: "Well, this then explains why you did not have a grim feeling as did the rest of us on the 20th of August, when Pat and I were at CIMADE for our farewell party! Of course you had time to get used to the idea and you had it resolved in your mind."

Chuck: "After all, Eastern Europe was not Evdokimov's idea of Paradise, being a refugee himself from the Soviet Union, not so?"

Jacques: "It was perhaps just as well that it was he who told them that they were free to go: 'Yes, go and visit the Soviet Union–see for yourselves what it's like!' But the philosopher Evdokimov was not an anti-communist Tsarist ! His horizons were much wider–those of a White Russian but not of a Tsarist. Joachim Chissano admired him immensely, kind of like a *père de famille* as they had long talks together. He would be invited to come into Evdokimov's family apartment and they would talk about the world… philosophy…theology."

Chuck: " Several years later, in 1986, I met Pascoal Mocumbi in Geneva. He had become the Prime Minister of Mozambique and was on a working visit to the United Nations. There he told me that while the students–Angolans, Mozambicans (including himself) and others–were all together in Sèvres in early August 1961, the "Angolan MPLA people" in the group tried to persuade everyone to leave the Cimade center in Paris, for Ghana. They maintained that Ghana's president Kwame Nkruma had a plane ready to pick them all up to fly to Accra, but that the students were divided over such an action. Part of the reason was that the MPLA leader of the Angolan group was out and was recruiting–and thus not available to influence the group one way or another."

"Mocumbi said that 'the main reason the Mozambicans did not leave was that they wished to form a united front in Mozambique, around Eduardo Mondlane's early efforts to create what became *FRELIMO*.' So they stayed in Sèvres. According to Mocumbi, the French lawyer's role in persuading the students to go to Germany was not as important as the internal dynamic of the *MPLA*. Also, he said that some students who did leave for Germany wanted to come back to France–and did, although it was not advisable at the time, given that Maurice Papon–the former Vichy official–was the prefect of police in Paris, and Charles Pasqua the chief of the special police unit".

Visit by Bill Nottingham to Washington on December 15, 1961

Bill: "Robert Service received me in Office 517 in the old State Department buildings on Virginia and 22nd St, at 10h30 a.m. I presume that Edouardo Mondlane had suggested that I look him up if I went to Washington, so I had called for an appointment. There were other people with Mr. Service, about four or five. No particular questions came up, except about how we did it. They were excited by the whole thing. He knew at the time that I helped transport secretly 60 Angolan and Mozambican students from Portugal across Spain to France. He had been sent by President Kennedy to Switzerland to verify the situation and offer scholarships for study in the USA. He had been instrumental in sending Dr Eduardo Mondlane to Paris, whom I met at Orly airport on August 17, 1961, and took to see the Mozambican students at Sèvres. The *FRELIMO* independence movement began at that time. When it was over, I said to Mr. Service, 'My passport expires this year. Will there be any difficulty to renew it, having been arrested in Spain?' He laughed, and said: 'Oh, no, we'd like to have you go back and do it again!'"

The archives at the John F Kennedy Library in Boston contain a memo from General Maxwell Taylor to President Kennedy dated July 21, 1961, saying that he had been informed of the president's interest in the students "who might request assistance for further schooling," according to a July 10 message from 'Geneva 31.' He said that the State Department thinks this would be unwise, because "the Portuguese authorities in Lisbon feel, rightly or wrongly, that the United States Government may have had something to do with these students leaving Portugal, and it might be impolitic for the United States to be officially associated with their further education in Europe or in the United States.

They, therefore, lean towards some indirect method of assistance if this should become necessary." Maxwell Taylor was Military Representative to the President.

OFFICIAL USE ONLY

THE WHITE HOUSE
WASHINGTON

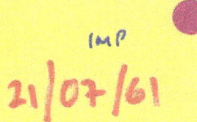

21/07/61

21 July 1961

MEMORANDUM FOR THE PRESIDENT

SUBJECT: Angolese Students in France and Switzerland

You requested that I look into the problem of Angolese students formerly studying in Portugal who have sought asylum in France and Switzerland and might request assistance for further schooling. (State Department message from Geneva 31, 7/10/61, attached.)

I have informed the State Department of your interest. They have asked me to point out that so far the Angolese students have not requested any assistance, either from religious groups which are in touch with them or from United States authorities. However, the State Department is in touch with these religious organizations and is prepared to do whatever seems desirable and necessary.

As to financing support for the students from Point IV funds, the State Department feels this would be unwise. The Portuguese authorities in Lisbon feel, rightly or wrongly, that the United States Government may have had something to do with these students leaving Portugal, and it might be impolitic for the United States to be officially associated with their further education in Europe or the United States. They, therefore, lean towards some indirect method of assistance if this should become necessary.

The Department of State will keep me informed and will give you a report before taking any significant steps.

Maxwell D. Taylor

Att: Msg fm Geneva 31
    7/10/61

OFFICIAL USE ONLY

July 1963 World Conference on Food, Washington, D.C.

Jacques: "In 1963–while the first meeting of the Angolans was going on in Massy, CIMADE's new student and refugee center outside Paris–I was in Washington D.C. for a World Conference on Food, initiated by the US government. I was a participant in the French delegation and was elected there to be one of the four vice-presidents of the conference. Of course the principle figure was that of the honorary president of the conference, who was none other than John Kennedy, then president of the USA. Kennedy was concerned about the world food crisis and had taken the initiative, via this conference, to mobilize public opinion as well as private and governmental organizations on the issue. Each of the four vice-presidents represented a specific sector of commitment. Mine was the sector of Non-Governmental- Organizations (NGO). The USA was not anti-French then and did not oppose a French nominee!"

Chuck: " Jacqueline Kennedy did travel frequently to Paris ..."

Bill: "And how!"

Jacques: "The French delegation fought hard to have a Frenchman elected ... So to have them choose a French Huguenot, certainly not in the sociological majority of the country–that was quite something!"

At the White House

Jacques: "Anyway, after one day's hard work, when I returned to my hotel –which was located not far from the White House–a well-dressed man was waiting for me in the lobby. He introduced himself as 'an advisor to the White House' and said, "We would be very interested to meet you personally regarding the problem of the liberation of the Portuguese in which you were involved'. I tried to deflect this question by replying that 'I am here for the meeting of the World Food Conference–that is completely different'. Yet he insisted, giving me an appointment at the 'Deputy Office' in the White House for the next day."

"Of course I went, but was circumspect on the details! On my arrival there were about ten people there: from the

Africa section of the State Department, from AID, from the CIA, and others. They promised me to give me a list and the functions of the participants at the meeting, but I never did receive it!"

Bill then asked whether the person from the State Department, at this White House meeting, was Robert Service, Africa Desk and possibly CIA, whom Bill saw in Washington in 1961. Jacques said he didn't know.

Jacques: "They were keen on receiving information on the operation. I was careful not to go into detail but confirmed that we, CIMADE, had assisted the Africans from the Portuguese colonies to flee Portugal and said that I was glad that some of them–seven or eight, as I remembered it– received scholarships to study in the USA following their arrival in France. In the discussions which followed, I made a point of underlining our obligation as Christians to assist the new potential leaders of Africa to prepare themselves academically so as to participate in an intelligent way in the freedom of their peoples (note the style of wording which I used ...). During my remarks I concentrated on the problems which the Africans experienced in obtaining scholarships and support towards these ends."

"In a second part of the interview the Americans wanted to know more about aid which should be given to the liberation movements. The use of violence ("terrorism" was the vocabulary already employed there) was raised. They were concerned about this issue because the White House, if I remember correctly, was in favour of supporting armed liberation movements, whereas the State Department was more prudent. The "White House" group, which represented President Kennedy at this meeting, was sympathetic to providing armed support to the liberation movements. The others were against."

"We also discussed the political situation within Portugal. They asked me: 'What do you know, through your contacts, of the actual political strength of Antonio Salazar?' I told them that I did not know much but that I was aware that, since 1960, the growing *'agitations'* of the liberals within Portugal were affecting its internal political panorama."

"Within this group there were certainly people from the CIA since there were insistent technical questions raised about any armed support for the liberation movements. I carefully pushed aside these questions since I was certainly no expert on the arms being used by the these movements! On the contrary, the point I was making was that we were involved, in solidarity, with encouraging and seeking assistance for the students' university education, through the YMCAs and other organizations. We were not about to divulge any sensitive information to Washington !"

"It was there that a representative of the Methodist Church 'admitted' having contributed heavily to covering the costs of the project, while Jack Kennedy was president at the time."

"It is true that the American support for Salazar and Franco had been diminishing during the Kennedy years. It was he who changed the direction of US support away from the regimes under these men. I made a point during the meeting that any support to Salazar was simply stupid and that one had to encourage something else for the future of Portugal."

"A fourth point brought up during the meeting had to do with Africa under the East/West Cold War tensions. I pleaded that aid from the West should be well-organized, coordinated and international in character, so as to counterbalance the Soviet efforts at that time. At the same time I said that I did not believe any more in a communist Africa than in an American, or French, Africa. Consequently, I said that we should push for the diversification of the scholarships sought for the African lusophone students".

"The role of the churches in all this was raised–both the policies of the churches as well as the practical and 'pro-active' initiatives and actions which they took. My remarks on this question constituted a class lecture on the responsibility of the institutional churches in this affair! I referred to both the churches in the US and Europe as well as those in Africa, including the fact that these latter are so dependent on Northern support.".

Chuck: "Clearly, hearing you tell of the contents of this meeting it appears that they were extremely interested in your sources of information, in the credibility of church sources and of CIMADE, as well as in the nature of the problems raised."

Jacques, thirty years later as an official of UNICEF, met Joaquim Chissano again in 1992 in New York. It was there, in a meeting where there were a small number of people, that Chissano stated (pointing to Jacques): 'This man is responsible for my presence here"

"CIMADE's action", Jacques commented "was no doubt a facilitator and accelerator of the decolonisation of Mozambique, but we were facilitators of this process because we contributed a certain number of technical means, our personal presence and the means to carry it out".

The key person in the operation was Pedro Filipe

As the representative of the Student Christian Movement (*la Fédé*) in Lisbon, Pedro Filipe's role was crucial in contacting the WCC, both in organizing the individual student members of the group as well as being the go-between with us and making sure that the operation went as planned. He was Jacques' first contact when he went to Lisbon in May and played a fundamental role in being the liaison person with the political leaders of the different movements. Pedro, Joao Vieira Lopes, Jacques and the others of the team were able to develop an indispensable mutual respect and confidence in each other. We had confidence in Pedro and he and the other students had confidence in us. Since then Pedro went on to become the regional coordinator for the UNHCR (United National High Commissioner for Refugees) for the entire region of West Africa.

Reflections

After it was all over, we all thought about this astonishing experience through which we were given the unique privilege of accompanying these courageous students out of Portugal and into an uncertain future.

"Maybe it was a weakness", Bill said, "but I relied on God desperately. This is why, for me, the events that we experienced cannot be conceived except in relation to faith. We had had the weekly prayer service on the Tuesday before we left, in the chapel at CIMADE's Parisian headquarters on the Rue de Grenelle, with the cross from the internment camp of Gurs as a centerpiece. We were not going to impose our ecumenical faith on anybody else, recognizing the predominance of Marxism for a large number at that time, but that was our situation. Prayer gave me endurance and–I suspect- the others also at times of emergency. There were crises every day. The emotion of crossing the border at Hendaye to return a second time to face the unknown was disheartening, but we kept going. I suspect every accident or near accident *en route* or scary situation evoked a flash prayer instinctively for each one. We had knots in our stomach or worse sometimes from our vulnerability and our dependence on a will other than our own. What could be our frame of mind waiting in Irun for the meeting with the Spanish authorities that would lead to interrogation and imprisonment? When we were in jail, we gathered for a time of singing but also to pray together, Catholic and Protestant, everyone scared to death that we would be sent back to Lisbon. With real fear and loathing we slept on those smelly mattresses. How could we not be grateful to God that everything turned out all right after so many close calls and chancy decisions both in Spain and in Portugal?"

"I came away from this operation", Chuck added, "with great admiration for the audacity and vision of this first generation of independence-minded Africans. The way they kept their disciplined determination intact during the harrowing trip from Portugal to France, in spite of the setbacks *en route*, remains strong in my memory to this day. The sacrifices which these men and women endured during the years immediately following the operation–some losing their lives in the independence struggle–can only merit profound respect, honor and the acknowledgement by their nations."

Participants at the 50th anniversary reunion in front of the
Cape Verde Presidential Palace with officials and guests

10

Fiftieth anniversary reunion in Cape Verde in 2011

In July of 2011 Pedro Pires, then President of Cape Verde, who had been one of the original 60 students to escape from Portugal in 1961, held a 50th Anniversary Celebration of the operation, inviting all who had participated to be his guests in Praia, the capital, for 5 days. It was called *A Fuga Rumo à Luta*–"The Flight towards the Fight". Fourteen of the original 60 students were present, as were Pastors Nottingham, Harper, and Jones, several spouses and other African friends. The five days of this anniversary celebration provided an opportunity for a joyous reunion and celebration of the *Fuga* and a series of meetings, held at the Piaget University in Praia. Experiences were shared in order to assemble a record as factual as possible of what happened during the flight and how it had directly affected the freedom movement in the Portuguese colonies. In those five days it became apparent to all present just how significant the events of July, 1961, had been in aiding this movement. Many of the escapees had wondered for fifty years who these Americans really were, who paid for all this, and whether the sponsor was church-related CIMADE–or the CIA! Two film crews, one from Angola and the other from Lisbon, were present to record the anniversary events. Hopefully the story of the *Fuga* will now be recorded and shared with a wider audience so that this small, but significant, piece of history is not lost or forgotten.

Fiftieth anniversary reunion in Cape Verde in 2011 103

Participants in the 2011 50th Reunion in Cape Verde see pictures of the 1961 Fuga for the first time.

APPENDIX 1
The list of the 60 African students in The Escape

Compiled by Charles Harper for CIMADE, in Paris, this list of the sixty Portuguese-speaking African students who participated in the clandestine escape from Portugal to France from June 16 to the July 2, 1961, had been divided into two groups which fled northern Portugal into Spain, and from there across Spain into France. Below are the names of the first 19 persons who entered France with relative ease. They were followed, two weeks later, by a second group of 41 persons.

The first group of 19, with each student's field and place of study in Portugal, previous to the Escape operation:

1. **† AFONSO, Vitor** — Angola
   Lisbon: Medical student

2. **ALMEIDA, Jeronimo Gaspar** — Ang
   Not indicated.

3. **† AMADO Romano Junior, Filipe** — Ang
   Coimbra: Sociology

4. **AMORIM MORAIS, Maria de Nascimento ("Ia")**
   São Tomé e Príncipe
   Lisbon

5. **BAMBA Idalina Augusto** — Ang
   Lisbon

6. **de CARVALHO, Job João Miguel** — Ang
   Lisbon: Theology/Journalism

7. **† FERREIRA, José ("Zeca")** — Ang
   Porto

8. **LOPES, Silvestro ("Cavacas")** — Ang
   Porto

9. **† MACEDO, Antonio Rebelo ("Certas")** — Ang
   Lisbon: Economics

10. MANUEL, Antonio
11. † MATEUS NETO, Joaquim Lourenço
    Porto: Political Science
12. † OCTAVIO, Fernando　　　　　　　　　　　Ang
    Coimbra: Medicine
13. PINTO DOS SANTOS, Antonio　　　　　　　Ang
    Porto: Engineering
14. da SILVA, Mateus　　　　　　　　　　　　Ang
    Coimbra: Medicine
15. VALENTIM, Jorge Lourenço Alícerces　　　Ang
    Coimbra: Political Science
16. VAN-DUNEM, Fernando José　　　　　　　Ang
    Porto: Law (born: 13.11.1941)
17. VAZ, Martins Filinto Elisio　　　　Guinée-Bissau
    Coimbra: Pedagogy
18. † WANGA, Jeronimo Elavoco　　　　　　　Ang
    Coimbra: Pedagogy
19. WILSON Eurico Oscar de Albuquerque　　Ang
    Porto: Medicine

The second group of 41

1. AFRICANO NETO, Antonio José Pereira　　Ang
   Coimbra: Medicine
2. de ALMEIDA SOBRINHO, Pedro Francisco　Ang
   Agronomy
3. ANTONETE, José Carlos ("Tony Aujoca Bi")　Ang
   Porto: Political Science
4. † ARAUJO, José Eduardo.　　　　Ang/Cabo Verde
   Lisbon: Law
5. de AZEVEDO, José Lima　　　　　　　　　Ang
   Porto: Economics
6. BELEM RODRIGUES, Francisco Xavier
   　　　　　　　　　　　de Carvalho e Rego　Ang
   Engineering

7. **BOAL Manue Rodrigues ("Tchaina")**   Ang
 Coimbra, Lisbon: Medicine
8. **BOAL, Maria da Luz de Andrade**   Cabo Verde
 Lisbon: History, Philosophy
9. **CARDOSO, Zacarias João**   Ang
 Lisbon: Theology
10. **† CARREIRA, Henrique Alberto Teles**   Ang
 Lisbon: Law
11. **CARREIRA, Maria Ilda Teles ("Baiana")**   Ang
 Lisbon: Engineering/Chemistry
12. **de CARVALHO SANTOS Henrique ("Onambwa")**   Ang
 Engineering, Geology
13. **CHAVES, Rodrigues Fernando**   Ang
 Porto: Business/Commerce
14. **CHISSANO, Joaquim Alberto**   Mozambique
 Lisbon: Medicine
15. **CHITACUMBI SANJOVO, Ruben**   Ang
 Coimbra: Pedagogy
16. **CLINGTON, Mario Alberto de Sousa e Almeida**   Ang
 Lisbon: Industrial Arts
17. **FILIPE, Pedro Antonio**   Ang
 Lisbon: Law
18. **FORTES, Armindo Augusto**   Ang
 Lisbon: Industrial Arts
19. **HURST, Jorge de Andrade**   Ang
 Coimbra: Medicine
20. **† LIAHUCA, José João**   Ang
 Lisbon: Medicine
21. **LIAHUCA, Maria Virginia de Graça Amorim ("Gina") + 1 infant, Nendela**   ST e Pr
 Lisbon: Nursing schoo
22. **LOPES da SILVA, Osvaldo**   Cabo Verde
 Coimbra: Engineering, Economics
23. **MEDEIROS, Antonio Aves Tomás**   ST e Pr
 Coimbra: Medicine

24.	MOCUMBI, Pascoal Manuel Lisbon: Medicine	Moz
25.	NHAMBU, João Jamisse Pre-Medicine	Moz
26.	† PAIVA JUNIOR, Fernando de Castro Porto: Engineering	Ang
27.	† PEDRO GOMES, Manue Coimbra: Medicine	Ang
28.	PEDRO GOMES, Teresa de Jesus Lisbon: Chemical Engineering	Ang
29.	PESTANA HEINKEN, Carlos ("Katiana") Lisbon: Medicine	Ang
30.	PESTANA, Elisa Bebiana Silva Andrade Lisbon: Nursing/History	Cabo V
31.	PIRES, Pedro de Verona Rodrigues Lisbon: Physics	Cabo V
32	RODRIGUEZ, Mimosa Custodia Pedagogy	Ang
33.	RUBIO, Carlos Osvaldo dos Santos Engineering, Economics	Ang
34.	SIMIÃO FONSECA Anna Francisco Languages	Moz
35.	TEIXEIRA, Augusto Lopes ("Tuto") Lisbon: Electronic Engineering	Ang
36.	VAN-DUNEM, Fernando José de França Dias ("Gégé") Porto : Law	Ang
37.	VAN-DUNEM, Margarida da Conceição Gonçalves Mangeira	Ang
38.	VIEIRA LOPES, João Baptista de Castro ("Bavil") Coimbra: Medicine	Ang
39.	VIEIRA LOPES, Virginia de Carvalho ("Gina") + 1 child, "Djoni" Coimbra, Lisbon: Languages	Ang
40.	VOSS FILOMENO de SÁ, Isabel Maria Medicine	Ang

41. **WILSON, Augusto Archer de Albuquerque**   Ang
    Porto: Engineering

The members of the CIMADE team who accompanied and transported the students named above from Portugal to France, were:

Within Portugal: **Jacques Beaumont** and **Charles Roy Harper;**
Within Spain: **Bill Nottingham**, **Kim Jones**, **Dave Pomeroy** and **Dick Wiborg.**

Chuck Harper, Manuel Boal, Bill Nottingham, Alberto Passos–a friend of the participants–and Kim Jones at Tarrafal, Ilha de Santiago, Cabo Verde, on the 50th anniversary of the Fuga, July 2011.

APPENDIX 2
What have some of these African students become since 1961?

Filipe **Amado** Junior: Parliamentarian in Angola
José Eduardo **Araújo**: Minister of Justice in Cabo Verde
Manuel Rodrigues **Boal**: Regional Director for Africa of the UN/World Health Organization
Zacarías João **Cardoso**: Bishop of the African Methodist Episcopal Sião Church, in Angola
Henrique **Carreira**: Minister of Defense of Angola
Henrique de **Carvalho** Santos: Minister of Industry in Angola
Joaquim Alberto **Chissano**: President of the Republic of Moçambique
Pedro Antonio **Filipe**: UNHCR Representative, African Region
João José **Liahuca**: A founder of the UPA/FNLA political party, Angola
Maria de Nascimento **Amorim Morais**: Foreign Minister of São Tomé e Príncipe
Osvaldo **Lopes** da Silva: Minister of Finances of Cabo Verde
Pascoal Manuel **Mocumbi**: Prime Minister of Moçambique
Fernando **Octávio**: Personal physician to the President, Angola
Pedro Rodrigues **Pires**: President of the Republic of Cabo Verde
Fernando Dias **Van Dunem**: Ambassador to Belgium and to the EEC; Minister of Planning; Prime Minister of Angola
Margarida Mangueira **Van Dunem**: Founding member of the Fundo de Solidariedade, Angola
Jorge **Valentim**: Member of the Central Committee of Unita, Minister of Tourism in Angola
João **Vieira Lopes**: Parliamentarian for the Democratic Front, Angola

Jerónimo **Wanga**: Parliamentarian for the Unita party, Angola

Nota bene:

The above list of 60 persons was established by crosschecking the primary sources of information contained in the archives of CIMADE based in Paris, with:

- the list of signatures of the 41 African participants held in the Spanish jail,
- the identification, by African colleagues, of persons in photographs,
- personal published memoirs, articles and interviews with the *Fuga* participants and others;
- and the lists of "escapees" established *post facto* by the Portuguese political police, PIDE.

APPENDIX 3
The participants at the 50th reunion in Praia, Cabo Verde

For the 50th anniversary of the FUGA, celebrated from 28 June to 3 July, 2011, in Praia, Cape Verde, fourteen (*names in italics*) of the former 60 lusophone African participants in the Fuga operation, as well as three of the accompanying Cimade team members*, were present–along with some family members, colleagues and other friends. The visitors were immensely grateful to the organisers of the event, and particularly to Hon. Pedro Pires, President of the Republic of Cabo Verde (one of the Fuga participants) and to all who hosted the event at memorable venues and in generous ways.

Pedro Rodrigues Pires
Joaquim Chissano
Fernando França Van Dunem
Margarida Mangueira Van Dunem
Pascoal Manuel Mocumbi
Alberto Passos e esposa
Amélia Araújo
Anatólio Lima
Terezinha Araújo
(daughter of José Eduardo and Amélia Araújo)
Ana Wilson
António de Santos Pinto
Augusto Wilson
William Nottingham*
Carlos Pestana Heineken
Carlos Nunes dos Reis
Corsino Fortes
Elisa Andrade Pestana
Charles Roy Harper*
Desidério Costa e esposa

Diana Andringa
Domingos Calvino de Carvalho
Eurico Wilson
Fernando Chaves e esposa
Howard Kimball Jones*
José Maria Neves
Margaretha Jones
Maria Helene Carreira (widow of Henrique Carreira)
Ikena Carreira (daughter of Henrique Carreira)
Luis Alves Monteiro
Manuel Rodrigues Boal
Maria da Luz Boal
Sara Boal (daughter of Manuel and Maria da Luz Boal)
Manuel Videira e esposa
Osvaldo Lopes da Silva
Paulo Lara (son of Lucio Lara)
Fatima Lopes da Silva
Rui Clington (brother of Mario Clington)

CPSIA information can be obtained
at www.ICGtesting.com
Printed in the USA
BVHW090903240719
554236BV00025B/1444/P